To the members of the median income group,
those truly forgotten men whose savings deposits
make banking, as we know it, possible.

Library of Congress Catalog Card No. 76-92024
SBN 910580-00-6

First Printing . . . . January, 1970.
Second Printing . . . . April, 1970.
Third Printing . . . . April, 1970.
Fourth Printing . . . . January, 1972.
Fifth Printing . . . . March, 1972.
Sixth Printing . . . . October, 1972.

DON'T BANK O

How to Make Up to 1
or More on Your Savi
All Fully Insured

By Martin J. Meyer
and
Joseph M. McDaniel,

Farnsworth Publishing Comp

TABLE OF CONTENTS

Introduction

In return for the use of his savings, the depositor not only has earned no *real* income from the banking industry, but he has actually suffered a *real loss*. Believe it or not, any sum of money deposited in any bank or savings and loan association at any time during the past ten to twenty-five years, after deduction of average income taxes on interest earned, would have bought more loaves of bread, more heads of lettuce, more rides on the subway or more copies of the Sunday Times with the original deposit than it will today with all of the compound interest added. Money must be made to multiply itself many times over in the span of a score years if the thrifty are to keep pace with inflation.

During the last two decades, business and labor have been able to increase their return, seemingly at will, restricted only by the laws of supply and demand. Labor, banded together, has forced increases in its returns, and business has been free to pass these increased costs, plus profits, on to the general public, the consumer.

It is not our purpose to condemn or condone the methods used by business or labor to improve the return for their contributions to our society. It is a matter of historical fact that both labor and management have been relatively free to chart their own course to greater returns, unhampered to a consider-

1

able extent by legal restraint. Nor do we argue either for or
against the reinstitution of wage-price controls as a means of
halting the inflation that erodes the value of our savings.

But we do maintain that a grossly inequitable situation exists
— unfair to depositors as well as to those who have invested in
life insurance or retirement annuities. Twenty years ago, people
invested dollars worth twelve loaves of bread. Today, each of
these dollars has grown (after income tax deductions on the
interest) to about one and a half dollars, a net increase of 50%.
But this dollar-and-a-half buys only *four* loaves of bread, which
means that you get less than *three* loaves of bread *now* for the
dollar that bought *twelve* loaves of bread when you invested it
twenty years ago.

During these years, the thrifty, in contrast to labor and
business, have not organized to work collectively in their own
interest; and even if they had, they would have run a collision
course with the governmental regulatory agencies that have kept
a tight lid on the interest rates that could be paid to depositors
by banks and savings and loan associations, despite the fact that
much of the savings industry had been willing and eager to
increase the returns it paid to its depositors.

The savings industry consists of three major segments: the
Mutual Savings Banks, the Savings and Loan Associations, and
the Commercial Banks. Each competes with the others for the
savers' dollars as well as for the borrowers' business, such as
mortgages, business loans and personal loans. Each of the three
segments are rigidly regulated: they are restricted as to the rate
of interest they can offer the depositor, as well as the extent to
which, and the areas in which, they can make loans.

These complex regulations have caught the loan-making
capabilities of the Savings Banks, and to an even greater extent
the Savings and Loan Associations, in an inexorable squeeze
between government-imposed restrictions, and the aggressive,
comparatively *un*restricted, competition of the commercial
banks.

Interest rates paid to depositors rise and *fall,* but, for example, only the commercial banks (of all the insured savings depositories) are permitted to offer their depositors *guaranteed* interest rates for periods up to fifteen years. Commercial banks can well afford to do this because they have almost unlimited avenues through which to lend out their money at very high rates of interest — avenues and rates that are at present prohibited to savings banks and savings and loan associations. These guaranteed interest rates compensate, in a large measure, for the regulations which prevent commercial banks from offering higher interest rates.

So it would appear that the depositor gets a better deal at commercial banks, not because of these banks' magnanimity or greater efficiency, but because they *must* do it to pry loose some of the funds that you, the depositor, have traditionally kept in savings banks and savings and loan associations.

If the growth potential of the commercial banks were to be realized, the eventual result could be the demise of the savings banks and associations. It would be the depositor who would suffer from the resulting lack of competition. It is to the advantage of depositors that each of the three segments of the savings industry, the savings banks, the savings and loan associations and the commercial banks, remain strong and able to compete with each other for our savings dollar. But there is no real competition among banks for these savings. Federal and state regulatory agencies prohibit banks from competing by offering higher interest. These government agencies set the maximum rates each type of institution can pay — but not the rates the banks can charge for the use of these savings dollars.

The time has come when the regulations of the savings community need re-examination to insure that the competition for the saver's dollar is free and uninhibited. Depositors must be able to get the best return for their dollar in a relatively free market place. That multitude of depositors who carry some three hundred thirty billion dollars to our savings institutions do so for many reasons, but one reason is dominant: to protect their purchasing power. Yet the sum returned to the depositor by the bank in the form of principal plus interest, after payment of income taxes on the interest paid, is worth less than the original deposit — less because of the loss in real value of the dollar due to inflation. Equity would suggest that no regulation or business practice should diminish the depositor's opportunity to have returned a sum at least as valuable as that which he made available to the bank.

But isn't permitting increased interest rates to depositors inflationary? It is. But, the claims of many administrations to the contrary, government has permitted inflation to burgeon — ever since wage and price controls were lifted after World War II. The millions of people who have saved a few dollars in the form of savings accounts and insurance have been prevented from gaining any profit from their investment — indeed they have been forced to accept real losses — by what amounts to government agency fiat. These depositors have contributed more, perhaps, to the growth of our economy than any other group, and it is unjust that controls apply only to interest rates to depositors, while there are no controls over the inflationary wage and price increases. Conditions permitting this twenty years of discrimination should be changed.

It may very well be changed by depositors acting *together*. This recognition of a common interest has been accepted by groups such as labor organizations, trade associations and numerous others. The savings industry has powerful, well-financed voices to state its needs and demands through newspapers, radio and T.V., and its power does not go unheeded in the halls of Congress and the offices of state and federal agencies. But the *consumer* has not effectively organized to make his collective strength felt. When the median income group, those truly forgotten men, have organized, they will have fashioned an instrument of great economic power, which, used judiciously, can advantageously advance their financial interest.

Until that time, though, the thrifty must do all they can *as individuals* to insure that the growth of their savings at least keeps pace with inflation. *Knowledgeable depositors have increased the return on their savings to eight percent, thirteen percent and even nineteen percent or more, while maintaining the safety of their funds through insurance by government agencies.*

The methods for making your money multiply through regular banking channels at higher-than-normal interest rates is described in detail in this book.

But to understand how you can use these methods most advantageously, it is necessary for you first to come behind the scenes of the banking industry with us — and learn why banks *need* your money, and *can* pay more for it. And why they *don't*. Unless *you* do something about it — individually or collectively.

PART I

Banks Can Pay More

Can the banking industry afford to pay higher rates to depositors? Recent developments indicate that commercial banks can afford to pay, and are anxious to pay whatever traffic requires. And what of savings banks and savings and loan associations? As you will see, many savings and loan associations as well as commercial banks aggressively promote some of the features that make interest rates around 8% possible. Quite apparently they want this money and are able to pay for it. Yes, banks can afford to pay more.

CHAPTER 1

Savings Banks --
They Save As Much As 14% <u>On</u> <u>You</u>

Savings banks tell us a good deal about themselves in their advertising. Take the *New York State Mutual Savings Banks,* for example. They're thirty nine billion dollars strong – thirty nine billion *depositors'* dollars strong. What do they have to say about themselves in their advertising? And what are the facts?

They *tell us* that at 5% money will double in fourteen years.

But *they don't tell us* that the chances of their paying 5% for 14 years are almost non-existent. Of savings institutions permitted to pay 5%, savings banks were among the last to pay it. If we look back at their history over the last twenty years, we can predict confidently that interest rates will be dropped at the first opportunity. And don't bet that savings bank interest rates won't go as low as one or two percent during the next fourteen years.

And *they don't tell us* that even if they do pay 5% ad infinitum, it would take *twenty years* to double your money *after taxes* (using the average depositor's combined Federal, State and City Income Tax Bracket of 30%). And in those twenty years, if the past can be used as a guide, while your dollars double, prices quintuple.

They tell us that they pay the highest rate on savings accounts of any type of bank.

But *they don't tell us* that for years, many savings and loan associations right around the corner from them offered ¼% more than the savings banks.

They don't tell us that many savings and loan associations pay 5% daily interest and give ten grace days every month while the savings banks paid only 4¾% daily interest and offered *no grace days.* Belatedly, starting April 1, 1970, the savings banks are anticipating 5% daily interest, but still offer *no grace days.*

They don't tell us that the insured bonds and certificates of deposit issued by commercial banks through January 1970 compounded 5% interest *daily,* giving a higher effective yield than the savings banks' 5% compounded *quarterly. They don't tell us* that commercial banks guaranteed their 5% interest for periods up to 14 years, while the mutual savings banks hadn't guaranteed their 5% for 14 days – until July, 1968, when some of the savings banks began to offer 5% certificates of deposit with interest guaranteed up to two years. But these certificates could not be cashed in on 90 days notice, nor on quarterly anniversaries, without loss of interest, but rather had to be kept until the predetermined date of maturity in order to have earned the 5%. And that 5% was simple interest—not compounded daily (which yields 5.13%). (See Figure 1, page 11.)

They tell us that mutual savings banks have no stockholders, and that all profits go to the depositors after deductions of expenses and required reserves.

But they do not tell us that no matter how high real profits might rise, these banks are not allowed by government agency regulation to pay depositors any more than 5%.

They do not tell us that when profits are in reality high enough to pay far more than 5%, these profits magically become "required reserves" that are in excess of the amounts required by the regulatory agencies.

Figure 1. Typical July 1968 Savings Bank Advertisement.

They do not tell us that these banks have built up tremendously high reserves from just such devices.

They tell us that mutual savings banks are people's banks. Once they were.

But *they don't tell us* that these supposedly mutual organizations are controlled by a handful of men, and that the people have no real voice or vote in determining the banks' policy and practices.

Today, savings banks are big business. They are big business with such powerful lobbies and public relations support that commercial banks, their prime competitors, have been prevented *by government regulatory agencies* from paying 5% on regular savings accounts!

They are big business with such an expensive and high-pressure advertising campaign, that many of us are seduced into giving savings banks our savings when we can do better elsewhere.

And remember, the millions and millions that go into this advertising, public relations and lobbying is paid for with money that savings banks have amassed from depositors' money. All the propaganda is paid for in full by the depositor from the depositors' earnings, under the heading of expenses.

And with these expenses, how could savings banks possibly afford to allow depositors a higher return?

To attract new accounts, savings banks mount advertising campaigns offering varieties of "gifts" in return for $25 or $50 deposits — sometimes even for deposits as low as $10 — provided the account remains for a year. These campaigns bring in hundreds of thousands of accounts, a good percentage of which remain only for one year. The banks are not permitted to pay more than $2.50 for these gifts, but the retail value is usually far more. What is the effective yield the savings banks are paying these depositors?

For a fifty dollar account for one year, the depositor receives

$2.50 in interest plus $2.50 in cost of gift (or about $4.00 in value of gift), to a total of $5.00 cost or $6.50 value. This is a yield of 10% measured in cost to the bank and 13% in value to the depositor! (See typical Savings Bank premium offer, Figures 2 and 3, pages 15 and 16)

For a twenty-five dollar account, the depositor receives $1.25 in interest plus $2.50 in cost of gift (or about $4.00 value), for a total of $3.75 in cost to the bank or $5.25 value. Here the yield is 15% at cost and 21% in value!

Add the cost of advertising the gifts, and of handling and mailing (estimates run well over a dollar an item), and you can see that the mutual savings banks afford costs of from 12% to 19%. Yet once you are lured by the "Free" gifts, they pay you only 5%.

As people withdrew their monies from savings institutions because better yields were to be found elsewhere, the regulatory agencies gave to the banks another tool with which to attract the unwary depositor.

Federal regulatory agencies and some state banking departments revised gift regulations so that by December 1969 depositors in such areas as New York were bombarded with offers of "Free Gifts of exceptional value" in return for new deposits of $1,000 or more. The "free" gifts included watches, cameras, luggage, electric can openers, knives, blenders, toasters, broilers, coffee makers, clock radios and vacuum cleaners – gifts that by regulation could cost the banks no more than $10.00 each.

Of the thousands of people who deposited millions of dollars into the banks offering the "free" gifts, all too many were unaware of the small print buried in the advertisements: I agree the minimum balance of this account will remain for 14 months." (Some banks required only 12 months.)

Many depositors did not recognize that, in effect, they were buying 5% certificates of deposit maturing in 12 to 14 months, with one added *dis*-advantage: They would earn the full 5%

only if they waited until the end of the quarter *after* the year
(or more) waiting period, since the 5% accounts do not pay
interest to date of withdrawal. All this in exchange for a $10
gift — and at a time when the chances for an upward revision of
interest rates were getting better than they had been.

Thus, with many millions of dollars newly frozen in banks
for a year or more at 5%, in the latter part of January 1970, the
federal agencies finally permitted interest rates on certain types
of savings instruments to be raised somewhat.

Savings bank interest on regular savings accounts was still
held at 5%, and on daily-interest accounts at 4¾%. But on savings certificates for 1 year, the interest rate was increased to
5¾% and for 2 years, 6%.

Those who were lured by "free" gifts were frozen at 5% for
at least a year — until the end of the quarter after the 12 to 14
month waiting period. Had they waited a few weeks, they
would have been getting 5¾% to 6% for their money at the very
same banks — still grossly insufficient to offset the real loss due
to inflation, but better than 5%.

Though the savings bank lobby may bend every effort to
have the doors closed to depositors earning 8%, you've seen that
savings banks pay *more* than that for the smallest accounts,
accounts that merit such rates the least. If, on the other hand,
the extremely large sums spent on savings bank propaganda
were added to interest rates, interest would be high enough to
offset the erosion of inflation.

Figure 2. Typical Savings Bank Premium Offer for New $50 accounts

Figure 3. Example of Savings Bank Premium Offer for New $10 Accounts.

CHAPTER 2

Commercial Banks --
They Tried To Pay You More, But
The Government Wouldn't Let Them

Only after World War II did commercial banks start to show a real interest in savings accounts. Their sales approaches were: convenience, services not offered by competitors, one-stop, full service banking. But their savings growth was slow, until Chase Manhattan pioneered the concept of *daily interest,* interest from date of deposit to date of withdrawal. Many people learned that lower interest (commercial bank interest has been about 1% lower by government regulation) paid daily on fluctuating accounts netted them *more* than higher interest paid only if funds remained on deposit till the end of a quarter. However, even this attractive new concept, successful as it was, still left savings banks and associations with the bulk of the country's savings. A brighter idea to give the depositor higher interest without violating the legal interest ceiling on regular savings accounts was needed.

It came from the Franklin National Bank and the National Bank of North America (then named the Meadowbrook National). Here's the background —

Savings accounts are the deposit instruments commonly used

by individuals. Business and governmental subdivisions, on the other hand, earn interest on their idle funds by purchasing certificates of deposit from commercial banks. These certificates are, in effect, instruments for the lending of money to banks for fixed time periods at a negotiated interest rate. Deposit certificates are available usually for periods of from 30 days to a year or more, and cannot be cashed in prior to the due date.

However, deposit certificates are negotiable and can be used as collateral for loans, or sold with minimal loss, should a premature need for funds arise. Interest rates on certificates fluctuate with supply and demand. Most important: deposit certificates were not subject to the maximum interest rate limit imposed on savings accounts by the Federal Reserve System or the F.D.I.C.

What Franklin and Meadowbrook did was brilliantly simple. They took certificates of deposit, waved a wand over them, and they became "bonds." They offered the bonds for long terms at guaranteed interest rates over the full term, but they could be cashed in on rather short notice. If the purchaser wanted income, interest would be mailed on payment dates; if he wanted growth, interest would accrue and compound at the guaranteed interest rate. And although Federal Reserve limited interest to no more than 4% on regular savings accounts, there were as yet no restrictions on what commercial banks could pay on their "bonds." So at a time when savings banks were offering up to 4½% (and S&Ls up to 4.85%), Franklin and Meadowbrook hit the newsstands with a big advertising blast — *5½% guaranteed!*

Before other banks or the regulatory agencies awoke, the two banks had corralled more than half a billion dollars. It was the most brilliant coup in the history of American banking. Franklin and Meadowbrook had stolen a march on the entire banking industry, vaulted themselves into national prominence, and started to give the depositor a somewhat more equitable return on his savings.

As money kept flowing in to the two banks, other commercial banks, large and small, defensively jumped on the bandwagon. But by the time they decided to jump, the two innovators had skimmed the cream off the deposit market.

The federal authorities moved swiftly against these banks that dared to give depositors a little more. Interest rates were rolled back to 5%. Contracts already consummated, however, couldn't be rolled back, so people who had bought the half billion or so of the 5½% bonds would continue to earn 5½%.

The rollback of interest rates, though, proved a boon to the two banks that had started it all. When competitors began offering 5½%, Franklin and Meadowbrook started to lose some of their deposits to the more conveniently located multibillion-dollar banks. Had interest rates not been reduced so precipitously, the two pioneering banks might have ended up with just a small fraction of what they had gained by being the first to come out with the 5½% bond. But the government acted so fast that the two innovating banks still had nearly $500,000,000 of 5½% bonds outstanding when the 5% ceiling was applied. The government action locked-in these funds, because depositors could only replace 5½% bonds with 5% bonds. From the day that issuance of 5½% bonds was prohibited, those who had already purchased those bonds would tend to hold them till maturity, since no other federally insured bank instrument offered an equal or better return until January of 1970, at which time interest rates on certificates of deposit were finally increased.

Despite the government-imposed reduction of interest rates to 5%, the commercial banking industry learned one important lesson. Though the thrifty may be creatures of habit, traditional savings institutions did not maintain their undivided fidelity. If commercial banks were to offer savers demonstrably more than savings banks, hundreds of millions of dollars of savings could be pried loose to swell the assets of business banks.

Again, the Franklin National Bank was in the forefront of the drive to offer the depositor more. It did this by keeping the certificate of deposit, or bond, popular with the individual saver. The reprint (See Figure 4, page 21) of their *Savings Investor Bulletin No. 1* mailed in January 1967, demonstrates Franklin's immediate attempt to recover from the federal ax applied to the 5½% rate.

While the savings banks were offering interest compounded quarterly, Franklin offered it *daily*. While their competition required 90 days notice for redemption, Franklin offered it *instantly*, after the initial 90 days required by regulation. And now one could buy bonds for as little as $100.

It is interesting to see how quickly Franklin changed terms to make the bonds more attractive. In the same envelope with *Bulletin No. 1,* the bank enclosed a two color order form, obviously prepared and printed before the *Bulletin.* The order form called for redemption only on multiples of 90 days after issuance. The Bulletin, a rush offset job, liberalized this requirement.

But again the regulators moved in, spelling an end to this liberalized redemption privilege. Franklin, by then accustomed to tribulation, rolled with the punch. Their next flyer went back to redemption every 90 days but offered bonds for as little as $19.47. (See Figure 5, Page 22.)

Another way to counter the restrictions of the government, commercial banks found, was to promote vigorously through hard-hitting advertising campaigns. A sound approach — but abuses crept in. Here's an example:

Some of the commercial banks were offering 5% interest compounded daily, with interest rate guaranteed for five or ten or more years. The ad men realized that 5% compounded daily yielded 5.13% after the first year, and an *average* of 5.26% after two years, 5.40% average after three, and so on up to 6.5% after ten years. (See Table I, Page 101.)

Ads appeared with 6.5% in bold type, and the small type explanation that the 6.5% yield occurs when the 5% is compounded for ten years. The statement of 6.5% was true;

FRANKLIN NATIONAL BANK

FRANKLIN SQUARE, N. Y. 11010

SAVINGS INVESTOR BULLETIN NO. 1

In the past several months a number of important changes have taken place in the savings market. Undoubtedly, the most important to you has been the regulation by the federal government prohibiting more than a 5% annual interest rate on savings by banks.

However, Franklin National is able to offer this 5% rate <u>compounded each and every day of the year</u>. In addition, we now <u>guarantee</u> your rate for <u>ten years</u>. (Only a commercial bank like Franklin National can do this). In ten years you will average 6.50% a year. Put another way, each $1,000 invested becomes $1,650 in ten years. You protect yourself from any sudden reduction in saving's rates for ten years. The answer is <u>Franklin National Savings Bonds</u>.

* You can withdraw your money (redeem the bond) at any time you choose after 90 days. And with full interest for each 90 days that you have kept the bond.

* Your interest starts the day you buy your bond whenever you buy it. Not just around the first of every calendar quarter.

* Franklin Savings Bonds can be held jointly or in trust just as regular passbook accounts.

* You can buy Franklin Savings Bonds for as little as $100 and in multiples of $100. And you can buy them by mail using the enclosed order form.

* Your savings are now insured to $15,000 by Federal Deposit Insurance.

A brochure containing an order form is enclosed with a post-free envelope so you may <u>act</u> <u>now</u> while this letter is still in hand.

Sincerely,

Figure 4. Franklin National Bank Letter, Savings Investor Bulletin No. 1

THE ABSOLUTE MOST!

The interest on your 5% Savings Bonds is computed each and every day. This is added to your savings. Next day the interest is computed and added to your savings again . . . 365 days a year, weekends included. This interest upon interest builds a return of 5.13% interest in the first year . . . a fabulous 5.68% yearly average if held for 5 years.

CHOOSE FROM 3 TYPES

INCOME BONDS — INTEREST PAID QUARTERLY BY CHECK. Minimum bond issued, $1,000 and in multiples of $100 thereafter. Non-transferable.

GROWTH BONDS — INTEREST ACCUMULATES TO MATURITY. Minimum bond issued, $100 and in multiples of $100 thereafter. Held to maturity — 28.4% in earnings! Transferable.

DISCOUNT BONDS — $19.47 to $7,788.14 per bond individually. In 5 years your $19.47 bond is worth $25 — 28.4% in earnings! Transferable.

Member Federal Deposit Insurance Corporation

Figure 5. *FNB Savings Bonds 5% guaranteed for 5 years.*

perhaps it was not meant to fool people, but it was misleading. Many people withdrew funds from the West Coast where they were getting 5¼% plus ½% from a money broker, and bought bonds under the impression they were getting 6½% per year if they kept the bond for ten years. (By the same ad men type reasoning, 5¼% deposits, if kept in and compounded for ten years, yields *much more than 6½%,* but they didn't stop to reason.) Reputable banks advertised 6½%, and 6½% many people thought they were getting. And, except for requiring that 5% be printed in type as large as that of the 6½%, the regulatory agencies have apparently not prohibited the practice, because it continues today. (See Figure 5A, page 24)

Innovation among commercial banks was not the sole property of Franklin and Meadowbrook. In the same era First National City came up with their own version of popularized bonds, another successful means for offering more than the 4% maximum limit on savings accounts in commercial banks. The device is called a *Golden Passbook Account,* and it's been widely copied across the country.

Basically, Golden Passbooks are certificates of deposit, but in the form of a passbook. They are sold or "opened" for minimum amounts of from $100 to $1,000. Additions of a minimum of $100, and at some banks less, are accepted, and ninety days notice for withdrawals is required. Some banks privately inform depositors that withdrawals are permitted without notice for any real pressing need. Recently, withdrawals have been permitted during the first ten days of each quarter without notice.

Since the start of the commercial banks' drive to capture a major portion of the savings industry, a see-saw battle has ensued with banks on one side and the combination of the House Banking and Currency Committee, the Federal Reserve and the FDIC on the other. Each innovation has been met by new restrictive regulation. But each new suppression has stimulated new ideas and offers. Even with all the controls and obstacles placed in the path of commercial banks, they can no

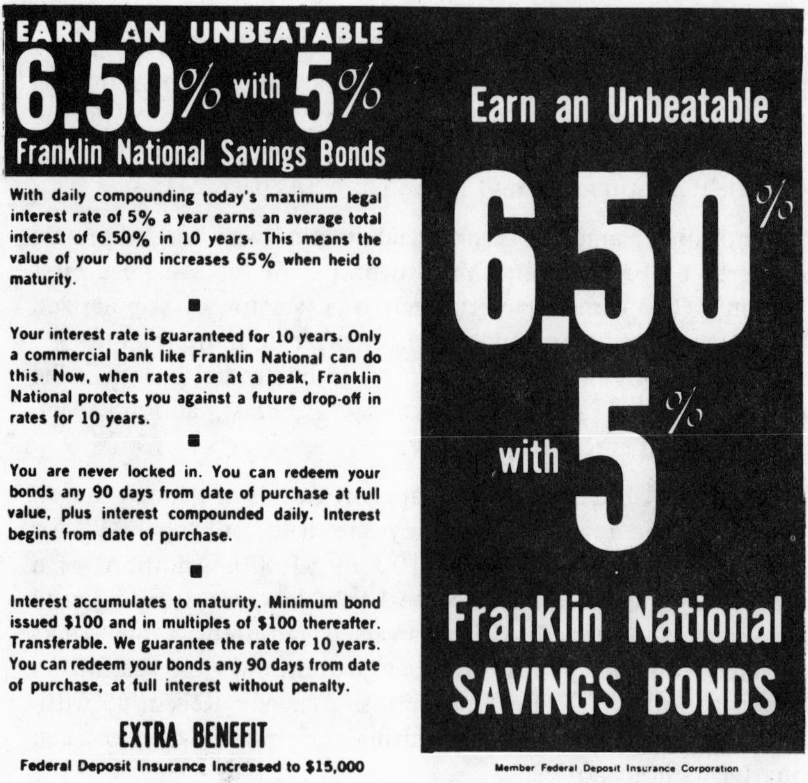

EARN AN UNBEATABLE
6.50% with 5%
Franklin National Savings Bonds

With daily compounding today's maximum legal interest rate of 5% a year earns an average total interest of 6.50% in 10 years. This means the value of your bond increases 65% when held to maturity.

■

Your interest rate is guaranteed for 10 years. Only a commercial bank like Franklin National can do this. Now, when rates are at a peak, Franklin National protects you against a future drop-off in rates for 10 years.

■

You are never locked in. You can redeem your bonds any 90 days from date of purchase at full value, plus interest compounded daily. Interest begins from date of purchase.

■

Interest accumulates to maturity. Minimum bond issued $100 and in multiples of $100 thereafter. Transferable. We guarantee the rate for 10 years. You can redeem your bonds any 90 days from date of purchase, at full interest without penalty.

EXTRA BENEFIT
Federal Deposit Insurance Increased to $15,000

Earn an Unbeatable
6.50%
with 5%
Franklin National
SAVINGS BONDS

Member Federal Deposit Insurance Corporation

Figure 5A – Franklin National Bank Advertisement

longer be considered an insignificant factor in the savings field. They've become big – real big; and it will take more than the archaic thinking of the savings bank industry to cut them down to size.

Just how anxious commercial banks are to be allowed to offer depositors a higher interest rate is demonstrated by a letter sent to depositors by the Republic National Bank of Houston. (See Figure 6, page 28.)

In response to the commercial banks' desire and ability to pay higher interest rates, the Board of Governors of the Federal Reserve System announced that effective April 19, 1968, banks that are members of the Federal Reserve System were permitted to pay 6¼% interest on 180-day time deposits of $100,000 or more. Ninety-day deposits earned 6%, sixty day deposits 5¾% and thirty-day deposits 5½%. Commercial banks were still permitted to pay only 4% on regular savings accounts. The various "bonds" offered by commerical banks were still limited to the 5% interest rate.

The effect of this regulation was that banks could pay 25% more interest to a 180-day $100,000 depositor than they could pay to a 180-day $99,000 (or $10,000) depositor. This 6¼% rate was readily available, which makes it apparent that the banks could not only *afford* to pay 6¼%, but were *willing* to pay it.

Finally, with the cycle of inflation going from bad to worse, and with banks "suffering" from a dearth of new deposits, the Federal Reserve raised the ceilings on certificate of deposit interest rates to 5½% for minimum terms of 1 year and 5¾% for 2 or more years. At the same time, once again the Fed permitted much higher rates to the $100,000 depositor – 6¼% for 30 days, 6½% for 60 days, 6¾% for 90 days, 7% for 180 days and 7½% for a year or more.

Both the April 1968 and January 1970 changes to the Federal Reserve's regulations (known as Regulation Q) would seem to be examples of discrimination against the great mass of people who, through their deposits, make the entire banking industry possible. It is directed against the very people who supply the major *bulk* of funds to finance home mortgages and consumer credit. It is directed against the people who have seen the real value of their savings shrink. It is directed against the millions who must rely on savings for their security. It is directed against the millions of thrifty people in favor of the wealthy few. And it is perpetrated not by the commercial banks, for they would quickly raise interest rates to all depositors were they permitted to do so. It is the fiat of an agency of a government of the people, by the people and *for the people.*

Yet, there is another side to the coin.

In many, if not most areas, savings banks and savings and loan associations cannot afford to increase their interest rates much beyond present levels. The greatest bulk of monies on deposit in these institutions has already been used to issue long-term, low-interest mortgages. A large percentage of their income is fixed by low interest rates that they will be stuck with for many years to come.

On the other hand, commercial banks invest primarily in shorter term loans so, as money has become tighter and interest rates have risen, commercial banks have been able to replace low-yield loans with ones yielding higher rates. In addition, the commercial banks issue business loans, personal loans, and various forms of consumer credit, including revolving credit and credit cards, areas of lending that yield to the banks double, triple or quadruple what home mortgage loans yield. These areas are forbidden to S&Ls and savings banks.

Were the Federal Reserve Board to lift the ceiling on interest rates for all types of savings deposits, there would ensue a mass exodus of funds from savings banks and S&Ls, because neither could match the interest paying ability of the commercial banks. Financial chaos could result. So there is a valid rationale behind what seems to be discrimination against the mass of the thrifty. But discrimination it is.

The federal regulatory authorities face a dilemma: who should be hurt? Perhaps the situation would be alleviated if both savings banks and S&Ls were permitted to enter the field of personal consumer finance. There is hardly a logical reason to permit personal finance to become the domain of only one segment of the banking industry, the commercial banks. Were the savings institutions to be permitted to make consumer loans, even though they would still be saddled with the old low-interest mortgages, income on current business would go up sharply. Another possible solution to the problem might be the extention of Federal subsidies to the home mortgage market. If it is in the public interest to maintain an adequate supply of low-cost mortgage funds, why should the thrifty be forced to subsidize it when other programs in the public interest are subsidized by the general public through tax-supported subsidies?

The real villain of the piece is not the Federal Reserve or the banks, but inflation. It is inflation that erodes the value of one's savings, making higher interest rates necessary. The victims of inflation are not alone the thrifty, but also the retired or pensioned, the poor, and everyone who pays to a retirement fund or saves for a rainy day.

REPUBLIC NATIONAL BANK
OF HOUSTON

5200 NORTH SHEPHERD DRIVE · P.O. BOX 10816 · HOUSTON, TEXAS 77018 · OX 2-6121

JERRY E. FINGER
President

TO OUR DEPOSITORS:

To dispel any misunderstanding on recent news releases regarding
increase in interest paid on savings, may I restate:

> "It is the continuing policy of Republic National
> Bank of Houston to pay the highest interest
> rate on savings allowed by governmental
> regulating authority."

Our current rate of 5% per annum interest on Certificates of
Deposit, Savings Certificates, and Golden Passbook Savings,
is at present the maximum allowed.

News items and advertisements offering higher rates refer
to savings in excess of $100,000.00 or more for six months
or more. We will pay $6\frac{1}{4}$% per annum on such deposits.

A copy of Regulation Q issued by the Board of Governors of the
Federal Reserve System is enclosed so that you can be completely informed.

We value your savings deposit very highly and pledge that
when higher interest may be paid, Republic will pay it.

Sincerely,

Jerry E. Finger

JEF/mbn
Enclosures

Figure 6. Republic National Bank of Houston Letter.

CHAPTER 3

Savings And Loan Associations--They Started The New California Gold Rush

> *"FREE!! 14 CUBIC FOOT TWO DOOR WESTINGHOUSE REFRIGERATOR-FREEZER WHEN YOU DEPOSIT $30,000 IN THE XYZ SAVINGS AND LOAN ASSOCIATION, BOOM TOWN, CALIFORNIA. OTHER VALUABLE GIFTS FOR SMALLER DEPOSITS. WRITE FOR FREE CATALOG AND INFORMATION!"*

Unbelievable? But true! This is typical of ads that appeared in the financial sections of metropolitan newspapers in the late fifties and early sixties. These advertisements started a chain of events that was a major factor in the real estate boom in California. It was the brainchild of one man and the initial cause of major changes in regulations governing the savings and loan and banking industries.

During the nineteen fifties the migration of multitudes of families to the sunny shores of California placed one of the greatest strains on native capital in a state that has ever existed in this country. Side by side with population movement was the growth of heavy industry, requiring building and more building, homes and more homes, apartments, stores and *mortgages, mortgages, and still more mortgages.*

Rich as golden California was, as financially rewarding as were its movies, its produce, its vineyards, local banking sources just couldn't come up with the mortgage money needed to sustain this boom in construction. They had to sell off parts of their mortgage portfolios to other financial institutions all over the country, particularly along the East Coast where banked money was more than plentiful. The Western institutions kept a portion of the income for servicing the mortgages, while the balance went to the banks that purchased parts of them. In effect, the Western industry acted as finder-salesman, service-man and bill collector for Eastern money.

In California, unhampered by usury laws which until 1968 in the East prohibited mortgages to individuals at interest rates in excess of 6%, mortgage interest rates soared. And on top of the high rates, many "points" or fixed initial sums were added to the cost. The California S&Ls decided it might be more profitable to lure some of the country's wealth to the West.

Throughout the rest of the nation, and particularly in the East, money — savings and demand deposits — was plentiful. Banks had little competition for the funds of the thrifty, so very low interest rates were paid. Through 1948, the New York savings banks were paying 1½%. The rates rose to 2% in 1949, to 2½% in 1952. It remained at that figure until 1956, when it reached 2¾%. Meanwhile, in 1956 the California Savings & Loan industry was offering depositors all over the country 4%! Note that 4% per annum yields 60% more than 2½%, and 46% more than 2¾%!

Yet even with this much higher yield, the great masses of the thrifty kept their funds in the bank around the corner. One reason: Eastern bankers spread stores that the federal insurance on S&L deposits was not sound. It is interesting to learn that no depositor ever lost a penny of insured savings there, even though a number of the S&Ls either failed or had such great financial difficulties that they were merged into stronger institutions.

The American Banker, *the* daily newspaper of the banking industry, in its January 24th, 1961 issue, had this to say in reference to the payout record of the Federal Savings & Loan Insurance Corporation as compared to the Federal Deposit Insurance Corporation:

"Closing of the $2 million Sheldon National Bank, In Iowa . . . made shocking headlines across the nation last week.

"In some ways the case resembles that of the Commonwealth Building & Loan Association of Portsmouth, Va. . . in 1956 . . .

"The Federal Deposit Insurance Corp., after an audit, will undertake to pay off depositors with amounts to $10,000 . . .

"It will take some time even before the FDIC can begin its initial payoff on the $10,000 accounts.

"But in the . . . [Building & Loan] case, there was no delay. The Building and Loan . . . was merged promptly into another insured association by the Federal Savings and Loan Insurance Corp. Its savings account holders thus were assured that their funds were withdrawable on demand. Of course, there was no problem with withdrawals.

"Such is the procedure of the FS&LIC when its member associations are insolvent or at a point where, if they were banks, they would have to close and await the liquidators. Since S&L accounts are insured to $10,000 and rarely have funds above such amount, the FS&LIC is automatically liable for the defunct institution in its totality. Its payoff can be immediate without risk of any savings account holder getting funds beyond the insurance ceiling as might be the case if the FDIC paid off all $10,000 accounts at once.

"Wherefore, the whole savings and loan industry, including individual associations and their national advertising organization, the Savings and Loan Foundation, can hammer away at the fact that "No one has ever lost a penny in an insured savings and loan association.

"We have pointed before to this contrast between
FS&LIC promptness and completeness, and the delay
and losses that attend closed bank liquidation because of
the laws under which the FDIC operates. For banking in
general, it is not a pretty set of circumstances."

The Eastern bankers' continuous campaign to undermine
confidence in the savings and loan industry through innuendos
about the solidity of its insuring agency, the FSLIC, had been
so widespread that Mr. Gaylord A. Freeman, then Vice
Chairman (Now Chairman) of the First National Bank of
Chicago, was recently prompted to state in an address before
the Illinois Bankers Association:

"Many bankers have sought to point out the difference between the insurance offered by the Federal
Deposit Insurance Corporation on the one hand, and
that offered by the Federal Savings & Loan Insurance
Corporation on the other. This effort is almost totally
without merit for there is virtually *no* difference
between the two types of insurance."

Yet lack of faith in S&L insurance kept many depositors
away from the California S&Ls. There were other factors that
deterred large-scale transfer of funds; doubts that funds could
be withdrawn when a depositor had need for his money, fear of
depositing in a distant unknown bank, inertia.

Further, as California raised interest rates, the East moved up
its rates defensively, always about 1% lower than the West, but
still up. (It is interesting to speculate what interest rates Eastern
savings banks would be paying were it not for the competition
of the growth areas of California and Nevada.) The West quickly
discovered that just raising interest rates was not a sufficient
lure, for each Western increase was followed by a compensating
increase in Eastern rates. This marginal increment, like a narco-
tic, kept the Eastern savings bank addict hooked.

But the inventive pioneers weren't licked yet. They turned to
the money-brokers who were able to offer offices and services
right at the doorstep of the Eastern banks. They paid the

brokers 2% on any deposits they would bring in, on top of their 4% interest rate. It was money they needed, and it was money they got. They recouped the 2% fee twice over by charging "points" and found no difficulty getting 7%, 8%, 9% for their mortgages. The brokers achieved a fair amount of success by advertising and offering personal service. Somehow, some depositors were more amenable to sending part of their funds three thousand miles away when they knew the transactions were handled by a local office.

But more money was needed. To satisfy this unfilled demand, the brokers turned to lawyers, accountants, union officers and anyone who could exercise some control over large funds, their own or others. All were offered "forwarding fees" for "recommending" accounts. Even pastors, priests and rabbis joined the financial parade. The fees given by the brokers ranged from ½ to 1 percent. The brokers were able to get thousands of people to act as their spare time salesmen. Some of this money filtered back to the depositors, some lined the pockets of the "forwarders." These part time salesmen brought millions to the brokers, and were paid in kind. Brokers operated openly, recruiting agents through advertising and direct mail. Equally openly, they paid the recruited agents forwarding fees or allowances for accounts they submitted or recommended. (See Figure 7, page 34)

But still more money was needed. The burgeoning economy of the New West had an insatiable appetite. In the Eastern banks, billions were lying fallow, while in the West builders and home buyers went begging.

Meanwhile, a small broker was struggling to make ends meet in his tiny hole-in-the-wall office on Manhattan Island. For some twenty years he had dealt with financial institutions as a mortgage broker, and more recently as an S&L money-broker. As a broker he received about 2% on any funds he could bring in to a number of California S&Ls.

And he had an idea.

Gifts for Thrift, Inc.

OF NEVADA

October 14
19   63

Dear Mr.

May we thank you for the new accounts or additions to
accounts recommended to the Insured Savings and Loan
Associations we represent.

Attached please find our check in the amount of $195.00
representing your forwarding fee.

Trusting you will find this satisfactory, and looking
forward to the opportunity of serving you again, we
are,

                              Cordially yours,

                              GIFTS FOR THRIFT OF NEVADA, INC.

                              Paul R. Gaynes

encl.   Paul R. Gaynes

Re: 9/10 - Mary   - $10,000 - 1/2 of 1% - $50.00
     9/12 - One Jeffer Ave.
            Corp. Geo.
            & Jack   - $ 9,000 - 1/2 of 1% -   45.00
     9/13 -   "   "   - 15,000 - 1/2 of 1% -   75.00

     9/10 - Victor   - $ 4,000 - 5/8 of 1% -   25.00

176 BROADWAY NEW YORK 38, N. Y. - DI 9-0270
SERVING SAVING INSTITUTIONS EXCLUSIVELY SINCE 1934

*Figure 7. Letter sent by broker to agent covering payment of allowance
for recommending savings and loan accounts.*

Why not offer gifts in return for thrift?

Not coin banks, atlases and shopping bags; but radios, televisions, washing machines and refrigerators. The idea developed into a plan, and in short order S&L ads appeared offering — *14 cubic-foot refrigerator freezers for deposits of $30,000! Service for 8 International stainless steel for $2,500! Write for free list of gifts!*

It worked: The advertisers were deluged with requests for the gift lists, all of which were forwarded to the broker in New York for reply. Inquiries were answered with ever expanding gift lists and the notice "If you have more than $10,000 and wish to have the names of other Insured Institutions paying the same high rate, write or call collect . . ."

By June of 1962, California interest rates had risen to 4¾%, and brokers represented large numbers of the savings and loan associations there. (See Figure 8, page 36.)

As a measure of the give-away program's success, the broker's hole-in-the-wall gave way to larger loft-type offices, and by mid-1962 "most gifts and prizes are on display in the worlds largest walk-in glass showcase," and gift lists were replaced by an attractive twenty page catalog.

By 1962 the broker, Saul R. Gaynes, confided that he was making more money than he knew what to do with. Gifts cost about ¼%, advertising and administration another ¼%, which left about 1½%. One and a half isn't a large percentage — but on a quarter of a billion a year it's $3,750,000! He had gained stock positions in a number of the Western savings and loan associations.

By his own appraisal, he was sending a quarter of a billion dollars a year to an area that sorely needed it, was raising these funds for the S&Ls at costs lower than any competing method, was helping tens of thousands of people to get a much higher return on their savings with government agency insurance safety, was supplying meaningful service to both the industry and the public, *and* was giving away to the thrifty absolutely

Figure 8. Typical list of S&Ls represented by broker.

free hundreds of thousands of dollars of worthwhile gifts. He was performing that age old function of moving resources to where they are most needed.

Any Eastern businessman remembers that this was a time when banks "begged" one to borrow money. There was just too much money in the East, and too little in the West. All the brokers combined were moving about $500 million a year to California, but without making a dent in the East's money supply. Everybody was winning. And Western needs were being filled.

Then several events occured to change the course of savings and loan history.

Despite the fact that Eastern banks, both commercial and savings, had more money on deposit than they knew what to do with, bankers resented this upstart "brokerage industry" that dared to steal away "their" money. — For, bankers view local depositors' funds as "theirs," their bank's property, — and anyone else gaining those funds is "stealing" what they take to be rightfully theirs. And banks have powerful lobbies . . . powerful enough to make federal agencies jump and State Attorneys General jump. Even the SEC got into the act.

The broker was in trouble. Agency after agency investigated his operation. Truckloads of his books and records were subpoenaed by the State Attorney General's office. And when he got them back, they were subpoenaed again, even before he had time to put them back in place. The harassment techniques were so effective that Gaynes' business and office became a shambles. Finally the broker's attorneys had to go to court to enjoin the state government agencies.

At the same time, more trouble was brewing in California. The S&Ls in California that were not in on the gift programs of Eastern brokers awakened. Local promoters, or the S&Ls themselves, started to offer their own gift programs *right in their own windows.* Those who have been in the Los Angeles area are aware of the proliferation of S&Ls — almost on every corner — and one more luxurious than the next. It's easy to picture what happened next.

John Doe deposited his dough in *one* S&L and picked up a T.V. In short order, he withdrew his savings, walked across the street, deposited it in another S&L, and walked off with a washing machine. From the next corner S&L he got a dryer, then on to hi-fi, silverware, china and a shiny new kitchen sink. The California savings industry was in bedlam.

The explanation of this disaster is simple. When one broker handled the gifts for many associations, the depositor couldn't deposit, pick up gifts, then switch to another freely. The broker insisted that funds remain put for at least a year, since he only received his full fee if they did so. But now this control had vanished.

The regulatory agencies in the State of California had no choice but to act. They prohibited gifts other than coin banks and printed educational material of nominal value. But the California prohibition did not affect the gift giving elsewhere, so brokers were still able to feed their hungry clients — the S&Ls with deposits and the thrifty with gifts.

To illustrate the magnitude of the operation, one S&L with assets of $14 million, retained the services of the broker-gift merchant. Within nine months the S&L's assets soared to $130 million.

Back in the East, the political pressure exercised by the Eastern bankers and their associations was intensifying. Finally, they got the legal action they were demanding. The S.E.C. held that brokers who had represented S&Ls anywhere without being Registered Securities Broker-Dealers were in violation of the law (despite the fact that depositors drew their checks and made their deposits to the S&Ls, not to the brokers).

This was a new kind of logic. Deposits in *banks* are not the purchase of securities, but deposits in federally insured *savings and loan associations* are! It's the logic of political pressure. Brokerage operations lost their charters.

However, they quickly registered as Securities Broker-Dealers and incorporated in more friendly states, still keeping offices in the Eastern metropolises. And the brokers kept on saving - saving the West Coast from financial ruin, providing the West Coast with the nourishment it sought.

More powerful action was taken against the brokers. On June 10, 1963 the Federal Home Loan Bank Board amended the Rules and Regulations for Insurance of Accounts to prohibit the giving of gifts, directly or indirectly, if the gifts cost more than $2.50. Further, no S&L was permitted to use the services of a broker unless they had less than 5% of their total deposits from brokerage sources. The Western S&Ls already had many times that percentage of deposits through brokers. The S&Ls were now effectively prohibited from dealing with brokers and from engaging in the successful gift programs.

The Federal Home Loan Bank Board's Resolution with its precipitate effective date — only four days later, June 14 — is reprinted in Figure 9, pages 40, 41, 42.

The brokers fought back. Prohibited now from giving gifts, brokers informed their clientele that "forwarding fees" instead of gifts would be forthcoming to them for accounts. Ostensibly, these "fees" were payment *for recommendation* of clients not in payment for deposits. These fees were upped to between ¾% and 1%.

"Points," or fee income charged by the S&Ls, were used to pay brokers for their services, generally at the rate of two dollars per hundred forwarded by the broker. In short order additional regulations were passed requiring the crediting of "points" income over a several year period instead of one, and increasing reserve requirements on increased deposits.

The restrictions were so severe that James R. Hambelton, in the December 16th, 1963 issue of the *American Banker,* under a Washington, D.C. dateline, wrote:

> "The Federal Home Loan Bank Board, in the face of strong industry resistance, is moving to brake the growth of the nation's $107 billion savings and loan industry.

Part 563 - Operations

AMENDMENTS RELATING TO SALES PLANS AND SALES COMMISSIONS

By Resolution No. FSLIC-1,591, dated June 10, 1963, effective June 14, 1963, the Federal Home Loan Bank Board amended Part 563 of the Rules and Regulations for Insurance of Accounts as follows:

1. Amend § 563.24 to read as follows:

§ **563.24   Sales plans; give-aways.**

Every applicant for insurance which uses salesmen, sales agencies, surplus certificates, or other sales plans shall submit, with its application, full details thereof. No insured institution shall, directly or indirectly, enter into, extend, or renew any contract, agreement, understanding, or arrangement that authorizes or permits any person other than such institution itself to promise, offer, or give a give-away, or to pay or absorb any of the cost of a give-away promise, offered, or given for or in connection with the solicitation, the opening or any increase of any account in such institution, or which authorizes or permits any person other than such institution itself to pay or to absorb any of the cost of any give-away advertising for or in connection with any such solicitation, opening, or increase; and no such institution shall accept the opening or any increase of any account for or in connection with which any person other than such institution gives a give-away or pays or absorbs any of the cost of any give-away advertising, or of any give-away given, for or in connection with any such solicitation, opening, or increase. An insured institution shall not, for the opening or increasing of any account, give for any one such opening or any one such increase any give-away that has a monetary value in excess of $2.50. The monetary value of any give-away so given shall be the cost thereof to the insured institution and the insured institution shall keep in its records for a period of at least two years suitable evidence of such cost. If the give-away is purchased or obtained by the insured institution together with, in connection with, or at the same time as another item or other items from the same supplier.

not identical therewith, such value shall be deemed to be the then current regular selling price or charge of the supplier on separate sales or dispositions thereof in the quantity included, and the insured institution shall in such case obtain, and keep in its records for a period of at least two years, a signed statement by such supplier of such regular selling price or charge. As used in the foregoing provisions of this section, the term "give" means to give, to sell or dispose of for less than full monetary value as hereinbefore defined, or with any agreement or undertaking, contingent or otherwise, for repurchase or redemption, whether total or partial, or to offer, promise, or agree to do any of the foregoing; the term "give-away" means any money, property, service, or other thing of value, whether tangible or intangible; and the term "account" means an account of an insurable type.

2. Amend paragraphs (a), (b) and (c) of § 563.25 to read as follows:

§ **563.25   Sales commissions.**

(a) *General provisions.* Except as provided in paragraphs (b), (c), (d), and (e) of this section, no insured institution shall, directly or indirectly—

(1) Pay any sales commission except to an employee of such institution;

(2) Pay to any employee of such institution any sales commission the payment or the amount of which is based in whole or in part upon the opening or increasing of any account or accounts in such institution, except a prize in cash or otherwise for participating in a new account drive or contest conducted by such institution; or

(3) Allow to any person any discount or rebate on or with respect to any account in such institution if the allowance or the amount of such discount or rebate is dependent in whole or in part upon

Figure 9. Reprint of Part 563 – Operations Resolution 591 6/10/63.

another person's having solicited or obtained the opening or increasing of any account or accounts in such institution, or enter into any contract or agreement under which any person other than such institution is allowed to collect or receive from any other person (except such institution) any compensation for or in connection with the opening or increasing of any account or accounts in such institution; or

(4) Enter into, extend, or renew any contract, agreement, understanding, or arrangement, which authorizes or permits any person other than such insured institution itself to pay, or utilize any device whatsoever pursuant to which any person other than such insured institution pays, any compensation to any person for or in connection with the solicitation, the opening, or any increase of any account in such institution or for any advertising in connection with any such solicitation, opening, or increase, or accept the opening of or any increase in any account in connection with which any person other than such insured institution pays any compensation to any person for or in connection with the solicitation, the opening, or any increase of any account in such institution or for any advertising in connection with any such solicitation, opening, or increase.

(b) *Exceptions.* The provisions of this section shall not prohibit any action which (1) is permitted by paragraph (c), paragraph (d), or paragraph (e) of this section or (2) constitutes the giving of a giveaway within the meaning of § 563.24 but is not prohibited by § 563.24 for the reason that such give-away does not exceed the monetary value (as defined in said § 563.24) which is permitted by said section.

(c) *Use of brokers*—(1) *General provisions.* The provisions of this section shall not prohibit the payment by any insured institution, within the limitations of this paragraph (c), of sales commissions to brokers, but no insured institution shall accept the opening or any increase of any account as a result of services of any broker or brokers or pay any sales commission pursuant to the permission granted by this paragraph (c) at any time when the outstanding balances of all accounts in such institution which were opened or increased as a result of services of any broker or brokers aggregate a total in excess of five percent of the total of all accounts in such institution at the close of the next preceding December 31 or the next preceding June 30, whichever is later.

(2) *Limitations.* Sales commissions permitted by this paragraph (c) shall be only such as are payable to a broker with respect to an account or accounts opened or increased as a result of services of such broker. No such commissions shall exceed, in amount or value, two percent of the amounts paid in for the opening of the accounts involved, in the case of accounts opened, or two percent of the amounts paid in for the increases involved, in the case of accounts increased. As used in this paragraph (c), the term "broker" means a person employed, engaged, or retained by an institution for services consisting in whole or in part of soliciting or obtaining the opening or increasing of accounts in such institution, except (i) an individual who is an officer, a director, or an employee of such institution, or (ii) an agent (as defined in paragraph (d) of this section) or a salesman (as defined in paragraph (e) of this section) utilized by such institution under circumstances permitting the payment of sales commissions to such agent or salesman under said paragraph (d) or said paragraph (e).

(3) *Maintenance of records; requirement of written agreements.* Each insured institution that accepts any account or any increase in any account as a result of the services of any broker or brokers or that pays any sales commission to any broker or brokers shall, in addition to maintaining such other records as will establish compliance with the provisions of this section, (i) before it accepts any such account or increase, and before it pays any such commission, identify each outstanding account that was opened or increased as a result of services of any broker or brokers, (ii) similarly identify each account that is opened or increased subsequent to the effective date of this section as a result of services of any broker or brokers, (iii) establish and maintain by a separate ledger control or otherwise a record which shows at all times the aggregate of the outstanding balances of all accounts that were opened or increased as a result of services of any broker or brokers, and (iv) make and retain an itemized record of each payment of sales commission to any broker, identifying each account and stating the amount thereof in respect to which such sales commission is paid. No insured institution shall accept any account or any increase in any account as a result of services of any broker or pay any sales commission to any broker unless such broker is employed, engaged, or retained

by such institution by agreement in writing, stating the service or services to be performed by the broker or brokers and the sales commissions to be paid, and the original or a signed duplicate of each agreement by which an insured institution employs, engages, or retains any broker shall be retained by such institution.

3. Amend paragraph (a) of § 563.26 as follows:

§ 563.26 Sales commissions; definitions.

As used in § 563.25 and in this section—
(a) The following terms have the following meanings: (1) "account" means any share, investment certificate, deposit, or savings account in an institution; (2) "compensation" means any salary, fee, commission, or other compensation, whether in the form of money, property, or otherwise; (3) "employee" except where used in paragraph (c) of § 563.25 means, and where so used includes, an individual (other than an individual who is a director of such institution) who is employed by an institution at the principal office or at another office of such institution and performs no services for such institution outside the regular lending area of such institution; (4) "officer" means the president, a vice-president, the secretary, or the treasurer of an institution; (5) "regular lending area" means the territory within fifty miles of an institution's principal office and the territory within which such institution was, within the meaning of the first sentence of § 563.9, operating on June 27, 1934; and (6) "sales commission" means any compensation which in whole or in part is compensation for soliciting or obtaining the opening or increasing of an account or accounts in an insured institution or any compensation by an insured institution to a person engaged in whole or in part in soliciting or obtaining the opening or increasing of accounts in any such institution; and

(Secs. 402, 403, 48 Stat. 1256, 1257, as amended; 12 U.S.C. 1725, 1726, Reorg. Plan No. 3 of 1947, 12 F.R. 4981, 3 CFR, 1947 Supp.)

"The board will . . . [issue] a controversial regulation to impose stiff, new reserve requirements on S&Ls. This rule will link reserves to savings shares so that the faster these increase, the reserve bite becomes proportionately larger.

"No single act of the board in recent years has stirred such a furor in the S&L industry as the new reserve rule. The reason for the fuss is simple. Some 200 to 300 S&Ls will have to cut dividends next year as reserve allocations absorb earnings that otherwise would be paid out to savers; another 500 or so will fall under the virtual control of the FHLBB, for they will need the board's permission to continue paying even modest dividends . . .

"The new rule reaffirms the present system of setting aside 10% of net income for reserve. Its curb on growth appears in a clause which provides that if an S&L rings up better than a 10% gain in savings in a year, the gain from 10% to 20% of total savings must be margined at 8% — not of net income, but what is far more severe — of the increase itself. Any gain above 20% will require reserve allocations of 9% of the savings increase; this, of course, on top of the first 10% and the next 8%.

"The industry is incensed with this rule. Feelings are running so high that even S&L men who usually are stong supporters of FHLBB Chairman Joseph P. McMurray's efforts to curb excesses in the industry are bitterly disappointed that he is imposing the rule in light of what they consider to be indisputable statistical evidence of its potential for damage . . . .

"For his part, Mr. McMurray has been saying all along that he was not out to penalize most S&Ls, that he will grant exemptions, waiving the new rule for what he considers financially sound, prudently managed institutions.

"As much as the rule itself, this notion of being subject to a waiver from Washington angers responsible S&L men in this part of the country who never have been accused of paying extravagant rates, or reaching for risky loans — charges Mr. McMurray has leveled at some West Coast Operators.

"Not only would the waivers be administratively cumbersome, eastern S&L men say, but there is deep resentment at having the conduct of their business subject to the whim of a government agency, particularly when there is no question of unsound lending policies.

"The new fee rule requires that closing fees, premiums and the like be amortized over several years rather than flowed through to the earnings of a single year, a device some S&Ls in the West use to inflate their earnings artificially.

"A study of the fee rule made by Julian R. Fleischmann, president of New York's Ninth Federal Savings & Loan Association, indicates the fee ruling will reduce rather sharply earnings in the West, while having a negligible effect in the East.

"Mr. Fleischmann's study, based on operating averages for state-chartered S&Ls in New York and California, shows that some $1.61 of each $6.67 earned per $100 of savings in California comes from fees, premiums, etc., associated with closing deals; only 28 cents of each $4.59 of net income per $100 of savings in New York comes from these sources.

"The new fee rule slices the annual return from fees per $100 of savings to 81 cents in California, but to only 21 cents in New York. Thus, Mr. Fleischmann insists, the fee rules will put California associations under heavy pressure, without disrupting the industry in the East. And it is the West Coast S&Ls that the FHLBB wants to restrict."

Figure 10, page *45*, a flyer sent out to a broker's list of clients, explains the fee ruling and makes obvious its effect upon both the broker's income and the "forwarding fees" he could then afford to pay.

In an attempt to roll with the punch, brokers accepted sharply reduced fees from the S&Ls, and agreed to accept payment over extended periods of time. Even the ruse of "forwarding fees" was ruled taboo, so the brokers attempted to employ their clientele as "community representatives." (See Figure 11, page 46.)

American Banker
New FHLBB Regulation Will Require S&Ls To Defer Fee Income Over 7-Year Period

WASHINGTON BUREAU

WASHINGTON.—The Federal Home Loan Bank Board has set Jan. 1 as the effective date requiring savings and loan associations to defer fee income over a seven-year period.

The new rule is designed to prevent associations from counting fee income as current income and then using the increased income figure to support higher dividend payouts.

In the board's view, the practice has been a factor in unjustifiably high dividends paid by some S&Ls.

The board's action came over the weekend with the publication in the Federal Register of its new amortization of fee income regulation. The final regulation is only slightly modified from the way in which it was first proposed on Oct. 23.

The new rule is the first of three steps the board has been studying to tighten savings and loan supervision, aimed primarily at keeping S&Ls from raising dividend rates to unsound levels. Other steps include tightening S&Ls reserve requirements and Federal Home Loan Bank advances.

The new regulation will allow insured savings and loan associations the alternatives of transferring unearned fees to a deferred income account or to a special loss reserve account.

FHLBB Chairman Joseph P. Mc-Murray, in announcing adoption of the deferred fee regulation, said the rule will have major impact only on that small minority of associations that charge "above average" loan fees.

Under the new rule an insured association can take into current income during the year, in which the loan is made $50 or 1% of the principal amount of a loan for the purchase of a new or existing house and $50 or 2% of the principal amount of a construction loan.

In either type of loan, an additional $50 in fees may be taken into current income when employees of the insured associations perform appraisal, attorney or loan-closing functions, according to the regulation.

If an institution wished to defer income under the regulation's alternative method, it would have to establish an account entitled "reserve for losses—Insurance Regulation 564, 23-1" and credit this account from net income with an amount equivalent to "acquisition credits" not deferred during the year.

"Acquisition credits" generally include other charges made by a lender for his own benefit but do not refer to average interest return on a mortgage loan.

The new regulation provides that the special reserve account be separate from each association's Federal insurance reserve account. As a result, transfers to the insurance reserve account will not be as part of the required transfers from current income to permanent reserves.

To our Professional Friends:

This reprint from the "American Banker" will better explain the reason for our revised "Forwarding Fee" schedules. It is urgent that instructions be followed carefully....

1. Checks and/or drafts with passbooks MUST BE SENT TO OUR OFFICE WITH INSTRUCTIONS FOR OPENING THE ACCOUNT. No fee credit will be allowed if sent directly to the association. POSITIVELY NO EXCEPTIONS.

2. Forwarding Fees are now 1/2% to 5/8%, depending upon the institution selected. Phone for special situations.

3. It is expected that accounts will remain for at least a year, or we will charge your account prorata. Fees payable in about 60 days after account is opened.

We are fervently hoping that the Federal Home Loan Bank will modify its rules which place Savings and Loan Associations at an unfair disadvantage with other savings institutions.

Cordially yours,

GIFTS FOR THRIFT OF NEVADA, INC.

Paul R. Gaynes

Paul R. Gaynes

Figure 10. American Banker – New FHLBB regulation 12/63.

But this attempt at avoidance of the FHLBB regulations ran afoul of the S.E.C. regulations. Savings & loan deposits had been ruled to be securities, and therefore community representatives were securities salesmen. As such, they had to become Registered Representatives of Registered Securities Broker-Dealers. The registration procedure was complicated and costly, and though the brokers tried, the clients in the main wouldn't go through the trouble. (See Figure 12, page 47.)

The series of changes in regulations were purportedly designed to inhibit or to slow up what appeared to be the too rapid growth of the S&Ls, decrease costs, render accounting practices more conservative, and insure the safety of depositors' funds. In practice, the changes accomplished their more basic purpose: the flow of money from East to West was brought to a dead halt.

Gifts for Thrift, Inc.

OF NEVADA

March 26, 1964

Dear Customer:

New Federal regulations have completely shut down all gift programs for the time being. We have many forces working for us to rescind these arbitrary rules which are an invasion of our Constitutional rights. However, so long as the law remains on the books, we shall abide by the regulations.

In order to enable us to continue to serve you and to spread the message about highest returns with Insured safety, we have carefully culled our list of customers and are wondering if you would care to become our community representative. We would put you on a commission basis and pay you a forwarding fee for all accounts you send.

Our policy has always been to represent only those Associations which are members of the Federal Home Loan Bank System and whose accounts are Insured up to $10,000 by an agency of the United States Government.

It has been a pleasure doing business with you in the past, and we sincerely hope that you will accept this opportunity for extra earnings. You will also do your friends and relatives a service by telling them about the $100 billion Savings and Loan Industry, which is more than twice the size of all Savings Banks combined.

Figure 11. GFT 3/26/64 New Federal Regulations.

OF NEVADA

Mr. William
325
Roslyn N.Y.

Dear Mr.

Dear Representative:

Attached you will find our check in the amount of $__79.30__
due you for the month of_____July_____as our registered
representative.

Your commission is based upon the following:

NAME OF ACCOUNT	AMOUNT	DATE	%
William	$21,146.73	7/2/64	3/8%
The amount with interest totaled Pio Bonds Bank Book	*21,766.43* *total $*	*Check should* *81.60*	

additional schedules on reverse side

We are grateful for your help in assuring the success of our
program to educate the public to an awareness of the values
of an Insured Savings Account paying the highest prevailing
rates in the Nation.

We look forward to an even greater, mutually profitable
relationship.

Cordially yours

GIFTS FOR THRIFT OF NEVADA,INC.

Accounting Dept.

176 BROADWAY NEW YORK 38, N. Y. - DI 9-0270
SERVING SAVING INSTITUTIONS EXCLUSIVELY SINCE 1934

Figure 12. Commission payment to registered representatives.

CHAPTER 4

Brokers -- They Win
A Battle Against Regulations

In the context of legislation that hampered the free movement of funds from areas of low return to those of higher yield, the broker performed an economic service — although often in a questionable manner.

To the brokers, the problem was survival in the face of what they took to be discriminatory regulation. Their solutions lay in avoidance or evasion. Many schemes were developed, some perhaps in the interest of the industry, all in the interest of self. For good reason they were out to perpetuate the S&L brokerage business, an enterprise that had supplied billions of sorely needed dollars to the West Coast and yielded profits in the millions to the brokers.

One thing the brokers recognized: their operations had to be conducted covertly. Were brokers to announce openly that they were giving gifts or cash allowances, they would place the savings and loans, as well as the regulatory agencies, on notice that the regulations were being violated. The regulatory agencies could effectively stop the S&Ls from accepting any business that originated with any broker who made such announcements, since that would be *prima facie* evidence that the depositor would receive some payment other than interest for his deposit. But the brokers didn't have to make public announcements to survive.

They had previously built up a clientele of well over one hundred thousand substantial depositors, whose accounts aggregated in the billions of dollars. In the previous years, by one broker's reckoning, more than 80% of clients' deposits remained in one place for well over a year. Less than 20% of the funds had been moved yearly to earn new gifts, allowances or commissions. The brokers recognized that they had a potentially powerful weapon if their clients could be motivated to withdraw and redeposit funds at the bidding of the broker. This proved to be an easy task. Brokers had already subtly informed their clients that cash allowances were available in lieu of gifts. (See Figure 13, page 51.)

Who wouldn't transfer a $10,000 account each year from one S&L to one of several recommended ones in return for a check for fifty to a hundred dollars each year — in addition to the earned interest?

But how were the brokers to receive *their* commissions? S&Ls were severely restricted. An ingenious scheme had to be devised. And it was.

The next step in the brokers' survival technique was to set up completely separate, nominally independent, but family-owned advertising and public relations agencies. Nowhere in the new regulations were there restrictions on how much S&Ls could spend on advertising, nor were they limited in their use of media. The savings and loans were free to utilize newspapers, periodicals, radio, T.V., and most important of all, direct mail and consultants.

The new advertising and public relations agencies, represented by the same old brokers, then approached the S&Ls with advertising deals. Considering that previously mutually profitable relationships had been built up and enjoyed, it is readily understandable why *some* S&Ls were willing to pay the broker-turned-ad-man large monthly retainers, and contract for expensive direct mail campaigns. Unwritten, was the under-

NEW ACCOUNT FORM
RECEIPT
WE ACKNOWLEDGE RECEIPT OF THE FOLLOWING TO OPEN AN ACCOUNT IN:

SOUTHERN CALIFORNIA
Savings and Loan Association   January 6   196 __8__

Los Angeles, Calif.
ENCLOSED PLEASE FIND:

Check ☐

Draft ☒   Investors S&L #00604 $14,900.00 ONLY

Passbook ☒   State Mutual S&L #0-123301-4   15,000.00 + Interest
        "   "   "   #0-123300-6   10,000.00 + Interest
        TOTAL $39,900.00 + Interest

Certificate ☐

IN THE AMOUNT OF __$39,900.00 + Int.__ . WITH WHICH YOU WILL PLEASE OPEN A

☒ Savings Account
☐ Investment Account
☐ Add to Passbook
☐ Bonus Account

IN THE FOLLOWING MANNER: [2] Individual   [1] Joint   ☐ Trust   ☐ Corporate   ☐ Partnership

                      ☐ Custodian   ☐ Pension   ☐ Other (See Remarks Below)

$14,900.00 ONLY $15,000.00 ONLY $10,000 + Interest
~~MARRIN AND HERR~~   ~~SCHOOL OF HEHE~~   ~~MARIN A. HEHER~~ OR
32 ~~Ashmood Road~~   ~~SCHOOL OF HEHER~~
Great Neck, N.Y.

MAIL ALL DIVIDENDS QUARTERLY

Interest from 1/1/68

PLEASE SEND   PASSBOOK [X]   DIRECTLY ☒

                                         TO US ☐

TOGETHER WITH NECESSARY SIGNATURE FORMS AND SELF-ADDRESSED ENVELOPES.

GIFT SELECTION: ☐ Allowance in Lieu of Gift ⟵

A. _____   ☐ Credit Account

B. _____   ☐ Taken

C. _____   ☐ To Be Shipped

Please Allow Up To 15 Days For Shipments or Allowances.

Gifts For Thrift, Inc. OF NEVADA

Serving The Savings Industry Exclusively Since 1934

176 Broadway, New York 38, N. Y.   Digby 9-0270

Figure 13. Broker's receipt to depositor showing optional allowance in lieu of gifts.

standing that the results of the "advertising" would produce deposits at a cost of 2%, or twenty dollars per thousand, or the same net price the S&Ls had previously paid the brokers.

Some S&Ls were then ready to operate with brokers as usual, despite the restrictive regulations. On the face of it, there were no violations. S&Ls bought advertising counsel and service from advertising and public relations agencies. The ad agencies "planned campaigns," but, for the most part, bought the use of mailing lists owned by the old brokerage firm. Thus far, there were no violations of law or regulations.

However, the regulations prohibit any payment to the depositor for his deposit and wasn't this a violation? No. Because the Federal Home Loan Bank regulations are governing *only* on the S&Ls, and on no other type of business. Brokers, or advertising agencies, or anyone else, for that matter, violated no law by making a payment to one who just happened to be a depositor. So, the depositor received his payment for his deposit from some advertising agency – ostensibly not for making a deposit, but under any other pretense. This paying agency was invariably a separate legal entity, not owned or controlled on the record by either the old brokerage firm or the new advertising and P.R. agency that dealt with the S&Ls.

The S&Ls maintained a posture of ignorance. And how could they know? They were buying advertising through an agency. The agency conducted a direct mail campaign. The agency bought the use of the best mailing lists available. That's all. The S&Ls remained officially unaware that a portion of the money paid for the lists then went to still another agency which, in turn, made payments to the depositors.

Now the brokers-turned-ad-men were ready to try their muscle. No one, not the S&L industry nor the regulatory agencies, foresaw the power of these relatively few men who exercised control over hundreds of millions on deposit.

Withdrawal requests had started to flood the S&Ls that had received deposits through brokers in the preceding years. The

S&Ls that had signed up with the new ad agencies for the "advertising campaigns" received enough in deposits to more than counterbalance withdrawals. But the S&Ls *that hadn't signed up*, received withdrawals far in excess of deposits. This created a potentially dangerous situation.

The liquid assets of the S&Ls involved are limited, as are the liquid assets of any type of banking institution. Limited also are the assets of the Home Loan Banks, and the Federal Savings and Loan Insurance Corporation. Yet when three quarters of a billion dollars which the FSLIC can borrow from the U.S. Treasury is added to these limited funds, an effective margin of safety is provided for the system under *normal* stress. But all of the assets and borrowing ability combined probably could not withstand any widespread panic.

And the only legal way the S&Ls could deter withdrawals might create a panic. By statute, when an S&L is faced with excessive, unmanageable withdrawal requests, it has the right to invoke waiting periods of up to six months.

The invoking of any such delay in honoring withdrawals, however, could precipitate a further flood of withdrawals, which would be markedly similar to the run on the banks during the thirties. One S&L falling victim to a run could be handled, a number of them subjected to a run simultaneously could produce a panic. And there just wasn't enough money to meet panic withdrawal demands.

California accounted for a major proportion of the country's S&L assets. A panic in the West could well have triggered one throughout the nationwide S&L industry. And a panic was a definite possibility.

To spell it out – had mass withdrawals continued, hundreds and hundreds of millions of dollars would have been removed from the Western S&Ls. The industry's liquid assets, capital and reserves, would have been insufficient to meet withdrawal demand, since an overwhelming percentage of the funds gained from previously made deposits were tied up in long term mortgages – assets, but not liquid assets.

Excessive demands in localized areas had been anticipated by the architects of the Home Loan Bank System, as it had been in the Federal Reserve and National Banking Systems. So the Home Loan Bank had moved in with loans to the associations that required funds to meet withdrawal demands. But, if demand had continued, the Home Loan Bank would have been hard pressed to supply sufficient funds. Had sufficient funds not been forthcoming, some S&Ls would have been forced to invoke the waiting period for the honoring of withdrawals. Such an action could well have signaled the start of panic runs on all the S&Ls in California, and panic in that area may have engendered a mass loss of confidence in the S&L industry throughout the country.

The "sitting-on-top-of-a-volcano" feeling was underscored by an unanticipated source. In a report sent to the Congress on Tuesday, October 6th, 1964, Joseph Campbell, Comptroller General of the General Accounting Office, raised questions about the liquidity of the Federal Savings and Loan Insurance Corporation, the insuring agency administered by the Federal Home Loan Bank Board itself!

The report stated that "serious situations" existed with some savings and loan associations which threatened to weaken the FSLIC. Since the middle of 1963 (which coincidentally was the date of the restrictive regulations passed by the FHLBB), the report continued, almost $62 million had been spent by the FSLIC to acquire assets of four savings and loan associations that had become financially unable to continue operations, and that the FSLIC may have to spend upwards of an additional $200 million if eight other "serious problem cases" have to be taken over.

The Comptroller General's report stressed that the ultimate amount of the losses that would be sustained by the FSLIC could not be estimated, because it could not predict how much of the cash outlay would be recovered in due time by selling off the assets of the sick associations, the assets being primarily home mortgages. The G.A.O. report pointed out, however, that the readily available funds of the FSLIC were threatened with serious depletion; thus the expenditures "could have a material effect" on the *liquidity* of the FSLIC, thereby placing the corporation in a "serious situation," which meant the entire S&L industry was in danger.

Where were the eight serious problem cases? Was it significant that the officials of the FSLIC failed to identify them? Some industry people believed that most, if not all, of the eight sick S&Ls were in Illinois, where there had been several failures and distress mergers. But by not identifying them, the FSLIC turned suspicion on California. Remember, the FHLBB's restrictive regulations were aimed primarily at the California savings and loan associations that were paying higher dividends than the rest of the country. The possibility of a panic was approaching reality.

At this explosive moment, Joseph P. McMurray, Chairman of the Federal Home Loan Bank Board, which supervises the FSLIC, and Norman Strunk, Executive Vice President of the United States Savings and Loan League, the major S&L trade association, jumped to the defense of the insuring agency and the industry. The defense pointed out that much of the payout money would be recovered through the sale of the assets of mortgage portfolios held by the defunct S&Ls, as had been mentioned in the General Accounting Office report. They estimated that 87% of the almost $62 million would be recovered. It was pointed out that the S&L industry's own reserves total $8 billion, and the FSLIC as of June 30th of that year had $1.2 billion available. Approximately 4,440 S&Ls covered by the FSLIC had assets of almost $109 billion, and that insurance covered almost $100 billion of savings.

It was not mentioned that the industry's $8 billion in reserves could not be called upon to support individual S&Ls that were in trouble, or that each $100 of insured savings was protected by only about $1.25 of insurance funds. Nor was the question raised what might happen to the FSLIC if eighty S&Ls were to collapse, since only *eight* failures might require $200 million of the FSLIC's ready cash. Eighty failures might cost $2 billion, a sum the FSLIC did not have.

However, the immediate defense of the FSLIC served an important function. It forestalled a mass loss of confidence in the federal insuring agency, the FSLIC. Without public confidence in S&L account insurance, the industry might have faced destruction. It was that close. No run ever developed on any S&L; no mortgage portfolios had to be liquidated. The few S&Ls that faced difficulties were quietly merged into larger and stronger associations, and no depositor lost a penny of principal or interest.

People connected with the California savings and loan industry always suspected that the repressive regulations were inspired by the East Coast banking industry. Yet this handful of men, the brokers, harassed by federal agencies and more particularly by the office of the New York State Attorney General, without the benefit of powerful lobbies and captive legislators, and with a hostile Eastern press, to a major extent managed to defeat the designs of those who attempted to throttle them and the Western savings and loan industry.

This precarious situation had been a direct result of the regulations which inhibited the actions of brokers operating in behalf of the California savings and loan associations. For had the brokers been able to service *all* S&Ls freely, the withdrawals in all cases would have been balanced. The chances of "sick" S&Ls, due to excess withdrawals, would have been eliminated or at least sharply reduced.

The crisis had made one thing clear. A few brokers had managed to put themselves into a position of power so great that without their cooperation, or with their active antagonism, the savings and loan industry in California stood in danger of collapse. And as California goes, so might go the nation of savings and loans. Look at what might have happened if the Board had decided upon strict enforcement of their own regulations.

Withdrawal requests might have snowballed to such an extent that the liquid assets of the S&Ls, the Home Loan Banks and the insuring agency combined would have been insufficient to satisfy account holders' demands for withdrawals. To raise funds to honor withdrawals, it is perfectly possible that the mortgage portfolios of the S&L industry would have to have been quickly liquidated. In such a liquidation, the mortgages could have been bought by the rest of the banking industry at a discount from its real worth. By then, any confidence in the S&L industry that may have remained would have evaporated. Withdrawals would have increased still more, new deposits would be non-existent. The assets of the S&Ls, the Home Loan Banks and the FSLIC could have been completely depleted, and the industry as a whole would have crumbled, with the commercial and savings banks falling heir to the whole mess.

Certainly the handful of men who comprise the Federal Home Loan Bank Board and its Advisory Council, saw these dire possibilities clearly – and that created a dilemma. Should they enforce their new regulations to the letter and risk the collapse of part or all of the empire they governed? Or should they tacitly permit the continuation of brokerage operations, in its then thinly disguised form as advertising and public relations? They chose the wiser course.

A deaf ear was turned to reports that depositors were receiving compensation for making deposits. To the same extent that passage of the Volstead Act inhibited the flow of alcoholic beverages, so Resolution No. FSLIC-1, 591 dated June 10, 1963, promulgated by the Federal Home Loan Bank Board, stopped the flow of payments, allowances, forwarding fees and other forms of kickbacks to depositors.

The brokers had won a great victory. It was also a victory for the nation's economy.

CHAPTER 5

Brokers -- They Get You More -- But Be Careful!

Although the regulations against brokers were never re-scinded, the authorities apparently chose to ignore them. To this day the operations of the brokers continue, not as formal brokerage, but in the guise of contracted advertising. There is one major difference.

Today, in a nationwide tight money market, interest rates are fairly well equalized across the country. Most banks and S&Ls, East or West, pay the maximum rates permitted by the Federal Reserve Board or Federal Home Loan Bank Board. California S&Ls no longer can offer interest rates higher than the rest of the country. Now, the only incentive for people from other areas to deposit in California is the under-the-table fee they can receive from a broker through some advertising agency. And the brokers have no way of informing the general public that such payments are available in return for their deposits.

So the brokers' clientele today consists mainly of the same hundred thousand or so people with whom they dealt prior to June, 1963, increased somewhat by word of mouth recom-mendations, and decreased by deaths and disenchantment. Whereas in the early years, brokers' clients earned much higher interest in addition to the gifts or fees paid by the broker, today they only receive the fee, and for that they must often wait long beyond the promised date.

Yet many hundreds of millions of dollars of Eastern money remain in the West Coast S&Ls. And through the brokers, the depositors transfer most of their funds each year out of one S&L and into another to earn a fee of ½% to 1% and recently as high as 2%. The total amount of Eastern money in California remains fairly steady; it is just moved from place to place every year. Each such movement brings a new commission, or rather a new "advertising fee" to the broker now-turned-ad-man; and, in turn, the depositor receives his payoff with each movement. During the past several years there has been very little growth potential for the S&L money brokerage business, but their operations have been steady and profitable.

The S&Ls used to pay for brokerage deposits and expected the bulk of such deposits to remain in their associations for years; today they pay much the same and recently much higher fees, but can only expect the deposits to remain for a year. Each year the S&Ls must pay a new fee to assure replacement of the funds they know will be withdrawn. Up to now, the West Coast has been willing to pay these new fees each year to keep the capital base of Eastern millions in California. But with the gradual slowdown of home construction in California, and the steady increase of native capital wealth, year by year the Eastern money is less and less needed. Eventually all of the money will filter back to the original source areas.

The same kind of ingenuity with which the brokers defeated the "California regulations," has produced other methods to circumvent the prohibition of financial or material inducements to depositors.

Here's one — for many years, mortgage brokers performed an important economic function by bringing together buyers — people in need of mortgages — with sellers, banks that have funds available to give mortgages. For this important service, the mortgage brokers were compensated by the buyer, the seller, or both.

Recently, some of the brokers forged an important new link in the economic chain by providing a similar type of service. Banks have made a practice of insisting that "compensating balances" of 20% or more be maintained with the bank if they are to accommodate business loans. When a business borrows $1-million, it pays interest on the $1-million, but it's only able to use a maximum of $800,000; the remaining $200,000 is required to be kept unused in the checking account as a "compensating balance." In addition to the interest charged, the bank is "compensated" for making the loan, *a compensation that effectively increases the interest rate charged by a minimum of 25%.*

Banks also establish "lines of credit" for businesses that require and merit such credit. For example, a business that has $1-million in the bank actually needs $5-million to operate. If the business keeps the $1-million in its checking account, the bank lends the business $5-million at an agreed interest rate, while the bank holds $1-million as a compensating balance, paying no interest on it. Often the business may have need for the $1-million, but cannot use it because it is tied up as a compensating balance for the $5-million loan.

In this situation, brokers saw the opportunity to perform a useful economic function, and profit from it. They learned that businesses with funds tied up in compensating balances were willing to pay to the broker between two and five percent, in addition to the bank loan interest rates, to arrange for the bank to lend the additional $1-million to the business at somewhat higher than regular interest rates. The broker does this by approaching the bank with the offer to supply depositors who will purchase $1-million or more in certificates of deposit at normal interest rates – currently 5% to 7½% for certificates depending upon maturity dates and size of deposit – as permitted by Federal Reserve's Regulation Q.

For the bank, this is a excellent deal, provided the business enterprise borrowing the money merits additional credit. The bank pays 5% to 7½% interest to the depositors, and charges about double its cost to the business for the loans.

For the business, it is an even better deal. Availability of adequate financing reduces cost of business operation and obviates the alternatives of costly factoring or other forms of non-bank financing. The premium the business must pay to the broker is small by comparison to the service he renders.

For the broker, the deal is the best of all — if he has the clientele who will purchase $1 million worth of certificates of deposit from the invariably distantly located bank.

So far, the entire process is sound. An important, constructive economic function is performed. Both bank and business stand to profit from the service of their intermediary, the broker.

But there is one link in this chain of finance that is weak. To induce his clientele to purchase certificates of deposit from a distant or "foreign" bank, since the interest rate is the same as can be obtained locally, the broker offers an inducement of a fee of 1% on small deposits to as much as 3% or 3½% on large ones, discounting the certificates of deposit to yield 6½% and as of early 1970, as high as 8% to 8½%. The individual is paid this extra fee by the broker. *Even though he receives no payments from the bank,* such payments by brokers to depositors for bank deposits are probably as much in violation of regulations as were the payments by brokers to depositors for savings and loan deposits. The process may be more devious, but the results are the same.

A word of caution: Federal regulations prohibit banks and savings and loan associations that are insured by either the FDIC or the FSLIC from giving directly or indirectly any financial or material inducements (except premiums that cost no more than $2.50 for small deposits and $10.00 for $1,000 deposits) to depositors or potential depositors in return for opening new, or adding to already existing accounts. Acceptance of such a monetary inducement may forfeit your insurance rights. Here's a case in point:

On March 17, 1965, the *New York Times* carried a story under the sub-heading "Suit Follows Bank's Failure," which reported that Gifts for Thrift of Nevada, Inc., a New York money broker, and its president, Paul Gaynes, were sued by Fred Geissen of the Bronx in Bronx Supreme Court. Mr. Geissen claimed that the money broker had opened two accounts of $7,000 each for him on January 11, 1965 in the San Francisco National Bank, which failed on January 22nd. Mr. Geissen charged that the broker "knew that the bank was insolvent," and asked for recovery of the $14,000 plus $500,000 in punitive damages. The complainant stated that he had made one-year time deposits at an interest rate of 4 ½ per cent, at that time the maximum rate permitted by regulation. What was not reported was that most, if not all people, dealing with brokers received or were promised a commission of about one and one half percent for deposits in the San Francisco National Bank.

The *Times* article reported that the Federal Deposit Insurance Corporation has *refused to pay depositors* in banks that had failed, *if the depositors had used the services of money brokers.* Geissen and the other depositors who had lost their savings apparently had no recourse. But there was something strange about the San Francisco National Bank scandal.

With reference to the charge that the broker knew that the bank was insolvent, the authors can vouch for the broker's innocence. In any deals with banks that later fail, the broker has the most to lose: not only his commissions, but the good will of his clientele – an irreplaceable asset of inestimable value to him. The broker, and other brokers all over the country were duped by the glib offers of the bank. Not only were the brokers duped, but according to the President of the National Division of one of the giant New York Banks, his bank and an even larger New York bank were similarly duped, one to the tune of about $300,000 the other of $2 ½-million.

The broker was innocent. But there isn't much question now that many people knew in advance that the San Francisco National Bank would fail. A subsequent Congressional investigation revealed many irregularities, including the removal of large sums from the bank *after* closing on the final day of operation.

The extent to which representatives of agencies of the government were involved in the San Francisco National Bank swindle may be deduced from some of the testimony taken during various legal actions. What follows is excerpted from the sworn deposition of A.E. Larsen, Regional Comptroller of the Currency for the San Francisco District, taken in one of the FDIC actions in the United States District Court for the Northern District of California, Southern Division, (Civil No. 43272, Volume III, pages 472 – 476).

> Q. So if you were asked the question which is the subject of interrogatory 34, namely:
> "State whether the last week of 1964 there was a meeting at the offices of the San Francisco National Bank at which there were present Mr. Saul Gaynes, Regional Comptroller A.L. Larsen, and some or all of the following: Thomas A. Berkely, J.W. Ehrlich, Edward W. Vodden, A.L. Johnson, H.D. Nichols, and Mr. Larsen's assistant, L. Butler." Your answer to that interrogatory would be "No." Is that correct?
> A. Yes, that is correct.
>
> Q. Did a meeting between Mr. Saul Gaynes and yourself take place during the latter part of 1964?
> A. Yes, I think so.
>
> Q. Where?
> A. In my office.
>
> Q. Were any of the gentlemen to which reference is made on Lines 31 and 32 of Page 12 of the interrogatories present at that meeting?
> A. I think they probably all were.
>
> Q. Who called the meeting?
> A. I think that Mr. Berkely initiated it.
>
> Q. Was it at or about the last week of December 1964?
> A. I think that is probably correct.
>
> Q. And it wasn't as late as January 1st 1965, to your recollection?
> A. I don't believe so.

Q. So if the words "Regional Comptroller" were substituted for the words "San Francisco National Bank" on Line 29 of Page 12 of that interrogatory, then your answer to the question would be "Yes." Is that correct?
A. Except that my name isn't correctly spelled, assuming it is I to whom they refer.

Q. Assuming that it is you to whom they refer, then the answer to the interrogatory would be correct, would be "Yes," with that substitution of "Regional Comptroller's office" for "San Francisco National Bank"?
A. Yes, that is correct.

Q. Now do you?
A. To the best of my recollection.

Q. Do you recall whether it was in the morning or in the afternoon, or over lunch, that the meeting took place?
A. It was not over lunch. That is to say, I did not have lunch with these gentlemen. I am not sure whether it was the morning or the afternoon.

Q. How long did the meeting take place?
A. What was the duration of time which the meeting consumed?

Q. Yes
A. It was not a long meeting. Perhaps half-hour, perhaps less.

Q. Did you know why Mr. Ehrlich called the meeting before the meeting commenced?
A. I am not sure that I did, although he may have told me when he made the appointment.

Q. When did he make the appointment, with respect to the time of the meeting itself?
A. I don't know.

Q. To your recollection was it within a day or two prior to the time the meeting commenced?
A. I would think so.

Q. To the best of your recollection, Mr. Larsen, what was said by the various individuals in attendance at that meeting?
A. Well, the meeting concerned the possibility of attracting new deposits into the San Francisco National, and this was going to be done, as I recall, to Saul Gaynes and Thomas A. Berkely.

Q. What do you mean, it was going to be done "to"
Saul Gaynes and Mr. Thomas A. Berkely?
A. I said, it was going to be done through them. As I
recall, Mr. Ehrlich had contacted them for this purpose.
I think the gist of the conversation and the purpose of
the meeting was to discuss with me the payment of a fee
to them for getting these deposits together. Then I think
to give me some assurance that they actually were
working on a project to attract new deposits into the
bank.

Q. Was anyone else present at the meeting other than
those individuals listed in interrogatory 34?
A. Not that I recall.

Q. Had you ever met Mr. Saul Gaynes prior to that
occasion?
A. I don't think so.

Q. Had you ever met Mr. Thomas Berkely prior to then?
A. Yes, I think I met him previously in connection with
a new bank application in which he was involved.

Q. But not other than that?
A. Not that I recall.

Q. You didn't have any meetings with him other than in
connection with that new application, I mean?
A. Not that I recall.

Q. Do you recall who began talking at that meeting
about the fact that there was a possibility of attracting
new deposits, through Mr. Gaynes and Mr. Berkely?
A. Not specifically, but probably Mr. Ehrlich.

Q. Did he ask you any particular questions concerning
the payment of fees? Did Mr. Ehrlich ask you?
A. I think so.

Q. What did he ask you?
A. I think he asked me to give the Comptroller's
position on the payment of fees to these third parties.

Q. The Comptroller's position, or your position?
A. The Comptroller's position.

Q. Did you do so?
A. I think so.

Q. What did you say?
A. I don't recall specifically. I may even have read the Comptroller's opinion.

Q. But in essence, in substance, what did you say?
A. That's about it.

Q. Well can you tell me what?
A. I have recited the Comptroller's opinion a short time ago.

Q. In these proceedings this afternoon, you mean?
A. Yes. I think that again was done in this case. Here again I'm quite sure I studiously avoided comment on the condition of the bank one way or another.

Q. Did Mr. Ehrlich ask you about the condition of the bank one way or another?
A. Not that I recall.

Q. Did any of the other parties in attendance at that meeting ask you about the condition of the bank?
A. I don't recall that they did directly, no.

Q. What else was discussed at that meeting, sir?
A. I don't recall anything else.

Q. Did they try to change your mind about whether or not fees could be accepted, or did they try to influence you to influence the Comptroller to change his position with respect to fees being paid?
A. No.

Q. Did Mr. Ehrlich know what your position was about the payment of fees prior to the time of the meeting?
A. I'm not sure.

Q. You don't recall ever having discussed that with Mr. Ehrlich prior to that meeting?
A. Yes, I probably did.

Q. If he did know it, what was the purpose of spending your time and everyone else's time for a half hour, when all of you were busy men?
A. Perhaps to give that assurance to Mr. Gaynes and Mr. Berkely.

FURTHER EXAMINATION BY MR. FISHER

Q. (By Mr. Fisher) Was the fee paid at this meeting?
A. What's that?

Q. Was the fee actually paid at this time?
A. No.

From this sworn statement, it can be inferred that not only were government agency representatives aware of the precarious position of the Bank, but that they did not make the brokers aware of the unhealthy situation. Mr. Larsen had testified "... I'm quite sure I studiously avoided comment on the condition of the bank one way or another."

A private interview with the head of one of the country's largest brokerage and advertising operations is of particular interest in view of the shadow that was cast over the agencies which have responsibilities for regulating and supervising banks.

The broker pointed to a pile of papers over a foot high, the results of his, and his agents, investigation. His clients had made time deposits, purchased certificates of deposit, and were not being paid out by the F.D.I.C. "Among those papers is enough evidence to hang . . . . and . . . . and . . . . There are sworn affidavits to prove them all culpable. They not only knew what was going on with Silverthorne [president of the San Francisco National Bank], they were in on it. Last week I took copies of it all to Washington and shoved it under the nose of . . . . He knew damned well that if they didn't pay off, I'd blow the whistle on them all — they'd all go to jail. Don't worry, I have . . . . 's word now that they'll pay out on all the insurance."

According to information available to us, this pile of evidence is in safe repose in some safe deposit vault, a potential political time bomb slowly ticking off the years.

Eventually the insurance was paid out by the F.D.I.C. to the full $10,000 limit on insured accounts. But only the President of the bank, Mr. Silverthorne, made the headlines. He took the rap for everything.

But no precedent was set. At no time was it revealed that the depositors had received fees from the brokers. It was only revealed that the brokers received fees, and payment of such brokers' fees are not in violation of the regulations, while fees to the depositors are. Even the FSLIC letter (see Figure 14, page 70) says nothing. It should be read carefully. There is no assurance therein that accounts are insured if the broker has paid the depositor directly or indirectly. It is not even implied.

The depositor must weigh carefully the advisability of placing deposits through brokers and receiving any fee as bonus. Should an isolated bank or S&L fail, the chances are good that no difficulties would be encountered in receiving FDIC or FSLIC insurance payments. However, should there be widespread failures, as was threatened in the S&L industry in late 1964, it is altogether possible that either or both of the insurance corporations would take the position that accounts opened through a money broker or its advertising agency are subject to question. Should the FDIC or FSLIC require, before paying out the insurance, a sworn statement to the effect that no financial or material payment was received by the depositor or his family, directly or indirectly from the broker, bank, agency or any other source, the depositor would be faced with impossible alternatives: he could refuse to sign such a statement and lose some, or all, of his savings; or he could sign and risk prosecution for perjury or possibly fraud.

If the FDIC or FSLIC refuse to pay, the depositor can complain to his Congressman, or even to the President, but it's not likely to help. These federal agencies, though sensitive to political pressures, are autonomous. Of course, you always have recourse to the courts for redress, *if* you can afford the cost and time. But even in the courts, you have no guarantee of satisfaction. The money broker gets you more – but be careful.

There are too many other ways to increase your return on savings to justify the risk of loss of federal insurance by using the services of a money broker. And these safe ways (described in detail in Part II) can pay you *up to 9½ per cent!*

FEDERAL SAVINGS AND LOAN INSURANCE CORPORATION

FEDERAL HOME LOAN BANK BOARD

WASHINGTON, D.C. 20552

———

101 INDIANA AVENUE, N.W.

OFFICE OF
DIRECTOR

March 16, 1965

In response to your letter of March 4, 1965, we may advise
that all types of withdrawable savings or deposits, including
bonus types of accounts, in insured savings and loan associations are insured by this Corporation up to the statutory
limit of $10,000 for each insured member in each insured
institution regardless of the name of the certificate used
to identify the account, the form (passbook or separate certificate) in which it is issued or the use of a broker in
its opening.

Sincerely yours

J. Kenny Lewis
Office of Director

Figure 14. FSLIC letter to depositors

CHAPTER 6

Commercial Banks Need Your Money--And They're Willing to Pay for It

---

Changed thinking, innovation and daring have brought the commercial banking industry to the threshold of attaining the greatest bonanza in the field of finance.

Try asking a bank *today* for a 30 or 90 or 180 day note (loan). Even offer collateral of triple the amount of the loan in insured passbooks and gilt-edged stocks. Or try asking one of them for a mortgage on a house you want to buy. Unless you are a highly valued customer of theirs whom they don't want to risk losing, chances are that you'll be turned down cold. But walk in and ask for the same amount to buy a new car, or to put a new roof on your house, and you won't be able to leave without their official check for every cent you need or want, even if you've never had an account with the bank.

It's obvious why one is turned down for certain loans, even if they are backed by more than adequate security, while a person easily obtains other loans, even without security. With a finite amount of loanable funds, the banks will place these monies where the return is greatest. On some types of consumer loans, the bank earns double what it does on business loans. On other types, it earns triple or quadruple. Consumer credit yields returns of as much as 69 percent per year. Yet, the commercial banks entry into this lucrative market was a comparatively recent event. Not too many years ago, if you had approached a bank to finance a pair of shoes, you would have politely been shown the door. The places for such "giant" monetary transactions were small loan companies, the Morris Plan and Provident Loan Society, finance companies, the neighborhood usurer or "shylock," and the local pawn shop. Banks would not deign to entertain such piddling business, and looked down their collective noses at the "peddlers" of consumer credit. The entrance into consumer financing was the first step in the "banking revolution" which is now under way.

That revolution means expansion of the banking concept, the introduction of new and profitable ways to *invest your deposits* for greater profits *to the banks*. This means the banks need *more* deposits (particularly in today's tight money market). They need *you* . . . more than they ever did.

Let's take a look at some of the *new* concepts that need your *deposits*. And then let's see what the bankers are doing to entice you to make those deposits.

At the end of 1967, the Bank Credit Card business was in its infancy, as were branch banking in the mid forties and certificate "bonds" in the mid sixties. Just as branches and popularized bonds have already been keys to growth of commercial banks, so will be the credit card and its eventual successor, the checkless or "less check"society. Banks are betting heavily on it.

As of October, 1967, according to Justin Watson, Deputy Comptroller of the Currency, in an address before the Northeast Conference of the Charge Account Bankers Association,

> "362 out of 4,790 national banks are engaged in credit card, check credit and similar revolving credit plans. The total outstandings were $656 million. There were only two states in the Union and the District of Columbia where national banks were not engaged in this activity. National banks located in four states — California, Pennsylvania, New York and Illinois — had outstandings of $397 million, or 60 per cent of the total volume. Pennsylvania, ranks second with $62.4 million outstanding. California led with $235 million, no doubt

attributable to the Bank of America operation, which at last year-end had 1,983,000 card holders and 64,100 participating merchants.

"It is estimated that presently bank credit cards account for about one-fifth of the estimated $5 billion in receivables outstanding for all types of consumer credit card plans. As of the last tabulation, 627 commercial banks in the country held $809 million. This tabulation includes only those banks handling credit card receivables and does not include several hundred additional banks operating as local agents of large city banks.

"Outstanding loans in the national banking system are approximately $130 billion. Charge account banking outstandings in the national banking system are $656 million. This constitutes only one-half of one per cent of the total credit outstanding in the national banking system. So I think you can see we have just scratched the surface."

Banks are so optimistic about the future of their credit card operations that they offer their card holders up to *45 days of interest-free credit*. An examination of the arithmetic of the charge operation indicates that the banks' optimism is well justified.

On an annual basis, Mr. Watson interpolated net loss ratios to be about one half of one percent with credit cards as compared to only one tenth of one percent net losses with general bank loan portfolios. At first glance a loss ratio five times as great as experienced with other loans may appear ominous. But let's see just how serious these losses of one half of one percent are.

To start with, on all credit card purchases, the banks take a discount averaging 5% before paying the merchant. So, after deducting the ½% losses, the banks are left with 4½% — and this *before* they start collecting interest at the rates of from 12% to 18% per year!

To put it in dollars and cents, on each $1,000,000 in sales via the credit card, the bank collects $50,000 in discount charges but loses $5,000 in bad debts. Added to the net figure of

$45,000 earned, the banks then collect 1% to 1½% per month in interest charges, which, on $1 million comes to $10,000 to $15,000 *per month*. Now add to this already attractive package, the various charges in addition to the 5% discount levied upon the merchant, and it all ends up as a highly profitable operation.

The ancillary charges made by the banks may appear inconsequential, but an examination of them is worthwhile. In a recent survey, a randomly selected sample of 250 normal-active cardholder accounts was studied. The results showed:

1. The average sales slip or credit-card charge was $16.03.
2. Such charges per cardholder were made 2.9 times per month.
3. There are 16 active cardholders to one participating merchant.

From this information, the following statistics can be deduced:

1. The average cardholder charges $558 per year.
2. The average merchant makes sales of $8,925 per year to cardholders of one bank.
3. The merchant handles 557 individual charges in a year.

In addition to the 5% discount charge, the banks assess the merchant for some additional items, approximated as:

1. $72 per year rental on a charge machine. (Of course, large stores need more than one charge machine.)
2. About $5 per year enrollment fee.

The costs to the average merchant for the $8,925 worth of credit cardholder sales can now be added up:

1. 5% discount charge on $8,925   = $446
2. Machine rental and enrollment
   charges total   77
                                                          Total   = $523

Thus, on $8,925 of sales, approximately $523 is deducted in advance, leaving the merchant with a net of $8,402.

Therefore, the cost to the merchant is not 5%, but 6¼%. Likewise, the income to the bank is 6¼%. Deduct the bad debt losses of one half percent, and the net income to the bank becomes 5¾%.

This discount and fee income of 5¾% is not 5¾% per annum. *It is 5¾ percent for fifteen to forty five days.* Then, after the interest-free or grace period, they collect up to 18% per annum on the unpaid balances.

Usual repayment terms are a minimum of 5 to 10 percent payment by the credit card holder per month, with a minimum monthly payment of $10.00. Taking an average bank credit card plan that offers 30 interest free days and requires repayment at the rate of 7½% per month at 1½% per month interest, and charges the merchant as listed above, some interesting figures are arrived at.

1. If *all* cardholders paid for all their charges on the last day of the interest free period, the bank's income on the funds used to finance the credit card operation would be 5¾% per month, or 69% per year, higher if cardholders paid their bills before the last day.

2. If *no* cardholders paid immediately, but took advantage of the maximum credit terms by paying only 7½ percent per month, the bank's income on the funds used to finance the operation would be something more than 25% per year.

3. Since some cardholders pay during the interest free period, and some pay in installments, the income to the banks issuing credit cards, *after deduction of bad debt losses,* should come to between 25% and 69% per annum on funds used by the banks to supply the financing for the charge accounts.

Since risk has already been discounted by having deducted for bad debts ½ of 1 percent from the banks' initial earnings of 6¼%, only amortization of original costs of going into the credit card business and current operating expenses need be deducted from this *25% to 69% income.*

From this examination of the mathematics of bank credit card operations, it is evident that this infant business will soon be a full grown giant. As of 1968, bank credit cards accounted for about $1 billion of the $5 billion in receivables outstanding for all credit cards. Total consumer installment debt is running near $80 billion, with total consumer debt, including installment debt, about $100 billion. Banks, through the mechanism of their credit cards, are aiming to capture a king sized portion of this vast total.

There is a resistance from sources such as large chain retailers that operate their own credit systems. However, the odds are good that the banks will eventually prevail. To finance their own credit card systems, retail chains often turn to banks for lines of credit — credit that has traditionally been extended for a fraction above prime rates. However, should the availability of these lines of credit be lessened, or should interest rates therefor be increased, retail business, however large, may find it impossible to continue in the credit card business. If banks can earn upwards of 25% by financing their own credit cards, why would they want to provide financing for competitive cards at one fourth or even one third that rate?

Along this rainbow path paved with credit cards, commercial banks are approaching the Checkless Society. It's a society, according to Dale E. Reistad, Director of Automation of the American Bankers Association, "in which we will use a proportionately smaller number of checks in the *funds transfer* process because we will have developed new, more convenient and economical payment forms which will replace many of the checks that now flow through the banking system." Computers and electronics will supply the means.

With electronic funds transfer, Reistad explained, in an address given before the Ninth Annual Conference on Electronic Data Processing, sponsored by the Retail Research Institute of the National Retail Merchants Association in September 1967, "instead of paying cash or writing a check to cover a consumer's purchase at a retail store, a consumer would be able to trigger a funds transfer mechanism which would permit the movement of funds automatically *without paper* — from the consumer's account to that of the merchant."

Electronic funds transfer could result in enormous savings to the banking industry. "Present forecasts," Reistad explains, "call for over 40 billion checks to flow through the banking system by 1980 (as opposed to approximately 20 billion items today). We are told that the average check flowing through the banking system is handled in 20 separate operations; takes three days to go from merchant to payee bank; and costs the banking industry 12 cents to process. If we can develop alternate systems which would reduce this figure by even 10 billion items, we are talking about a potential *savings of $470-million dollars* to the system, measured in 1967 dollars."

It is obvious that electronic funds transfer can be extended to credit cards since, in essence, they both serve the same function. As a matter of fact, the check and credit card have been so changed, improved, and merged that the difference in point of utility becomes indefinable. Reistad gave some examples:

"It was to be expected that banks would want to expand the 'check cashing privilege cards,' which enable a customer to cash his check in any of the bank's branch offices, to nonbanks, and they have done so by offering 'check guaranty' protection on checks cashed up to a certain amount by any area merchant.

"At the same time 'line-of-credit' plans developed connected either to the customer's checking account, his credit card account, or both. There are no significant differences between writing a check against a line of credit or the new 'do-it-yourself' travelers check — merely mechanical differences only of academic interest to the recipient merchant.

"Hardly a day goes by when there isn't some new variation upon the check or credit card theme being announced. *While cash is still very much in evidence, it becomes less important with each new breakthrough in payment system development!"*

It appears certain that consumer credit — made even more

profitable by the elimination of paper funds transfer through electronics — will bring an unparalleled prosperity to the commercial banks. But to achieve this bonanza, which is "in the cards," yet leave sufficient funds available to finance all their other operations, banks have to gain as high of a percentage of the country's savings as they possibly can. Their need for money is unlimited.

However, many restrictions block an easy path to this goal. Commercial banks until January 1970 could only pay 4% on their regular savings accounts, and were limited to 5% on the innovations they have created — golden passbooks and bonds. They *can* pay more to larger depositors. Since April 1968 they were allowed to offer up to 6¼% on certificates of $100,000 or more, and in January 1970 this rate was increased to 7½% on 1 year deposits. As of this latter date, smaller C.D.'s can yield up to 5¾% (for 2 year terms).

To overcome restrictions, the banks again have turned to innovation. Their offer of free credit for up to 45 days is just a starting point. "We hand our credit card to the cashier in lieu of cash with a feeling of inward satisfaction," Reistad explains, "because we know there will be a long delay before we receive the bill, which, if we decide to pay in full, will have meant free use of the funds for the elapsed period of time since the original purchase.

"Why then pay cash? Why pay when the merchant will accept a credit card arrangement in lieu of cash for 15, 30 or maybe even 45 days without interest?"

Why *free* credit? Consider: Ordinary mortgages and time loans that yielded 6% to 7% (and recently to 9%) before deduction of bad debt losses, are able to support interest rates to depositors of 5%. One can only guess how high interest rates would go with operations yielding 25% to 69% — *if* the banks were allowed to pay more than 5%. But they're not (except on long term C.D.'s.) So it's no wonder that they offer *free* credit for 15 to 45 days. And it's understandable why they've offered loopholes through which you can net more than 5%, and why the regulatory agencies have not plugged up these loopholes.

Commercial banks can avoid the 5% interest limitation whenever they choose by means of a simple device that has been in use for several years without interference from the Federal Reserve or other regulatory agencies. In practice, however, only about 40,000 people make regular use of this device, so it is not sufficiently wide-spread to arouse the mass opposition of the several powerful lobbies that exist to hold down interest rates to the thrifty. Here's the principle of the device —

A bank has the right to lend money without charging interest. Interest-free credit cards are an example. So whenever a bank wishes to give depositors a return on their banked savings of more than 5%, all they need do is lend the depositor interest-free money based on a percentage of his deposits! Too obvious a violation of the regulations? Not at all — because 40,000 people are now enjoying its benefits, and have been for some time now, and with the knowledge of the banking industry in general and the regulatory agencies in particular. Here's one way the device could work in practice —

1. An individual deposits $10,000 in a 5% Golden Passbook account or purchases a $10,000 bond.
2. If the bank wants to pay interest of 6¼%, not the 5% ceiling, the bank gives the depositor an interest-free loan of $2,000. The loan could be automatically renewable by mutual consent every 30 days or each quarter, and is fully secured by the $10,000 account.
3. The depositor therefore earns 5% interest on $10,000, to a total of $500 although he actually has only $8,000 in the bank. Interest of $500 on $8,000 is at the rate of 6¼%.

Another way the device could work —

1. An individual with $10,000 ready for deposit is given a $2,500 interest-free loan.
2. The total of $12,500 is then deposited into a 5% account.
3. Annual interest on the $12,500 is $625, but since only $10,000 actually is the depositor's money, the $625 interest on a principal of $10,000 is actually at the rate of 6¼%.

The commercial banks of the country have a pressing need for greater and greater deposits. Until other more profitable investment opportunities are allowed to the savings banks and savings and loan associations, only the commercial banks have the opportunities to earn the really high return that personal loans and installment credit offer. *They need the deposit money, and can well afford to pay for it.* They have learned that they can pay without violating any regulations, by offering interest-free loans.

It is just such aggressive, innovative actions that have made it possible for a few to earn up to eight or nine percent on their savings, and holds promise to the many that they may do the same.

CHAPTER 7

Why the Government Won't Let the Banks Pay More

Savings institutions, particularly savings and loan associations, were originally conceived to permit the pooling of funds so members of the group could build homes for themselves. There wasn't enough money for all to build at the same time, so some depositors had to wait. In return for their money, risk, and patience while others built homes, these depositors were repaid with interest. Sooner or later their turn would come to build homes. It was in the interest of all to keep the interest rate down, so the cost of the homes would stay within reach. It was not money the depositor was after. It was a home for his family.

The general concept of low interest rates has carried over into the field of mortgaging.

In order to keep home ownership within the possible realm of millions, in many states, governmental bodies with the legal authority to do so, have maintained ceilings on interest rates allowed to be charged for home mortgages. Low interest rates for mortgages have been made possible only through mandatory low interest rates to depositors — the thrifty. So, a few million mortgagees have profited at the expense of a hundred million thrifty folk — and all this by government regulation of interest rate ceilings.

The survival of savings and loan associations depends upon the retention of the low-rate ceilings. S&Ls are permitted to operate only within the narrowest of limits, and are almost entirely restricted by regulations to granting mortgage loans secured by residential real estate. Most of their mortgages are written for single family owner-occupied homes within a small radius of their base of operations. S&Ls are not permitted to invest in stocks and bonds, nor can they offer demand loans, personal loans or credit cards. Where states have no effective usury laws, mortgage lending by itself can be sufficiently profitable to permit S&Ls to compete with other financial institutions for the saver's dollar, *as long as interest rates to depositors are controlled.*

However, in many states, particularly along the Eastern seaboard, the savings and loan industry has been caught in an inexorable squeeze. As an example: through June of 1968, the State of New York, in which mortgages to individuals are covered by usury laws, prohibited mortgage interest rates to individuals in excess of 6%. It is just not financially feasible to pay depositors 5% and collect only 6% on mortgages. Operating and necessary loss reserve costs exceed this 1% spread. So the S&Ls were forced to give mortgage loans to corporations rather than to individuals, because usury laws do not apply to interest charged to corporations. This squeeze effectively removed the S&Ls from the private home mortgage field. (And this occurred in a state that permits banks and finance companies to charge individuals true interest rates of from twelve to thirty percent for other types of loans.) It is obvious that if interest rates on deposits were raised, S&Ls would no longer be economically viable — unless they were permitted to engage in other types of banking, or were subsidized.

Savings banks are permitted broader horizons than the savings and loans. Their mortgages run from home through business and industrial construction. Most of their mortgage funds can go into corporate owned large structures where interest rates are not subject to legal restraint. Savings banks also invest in stocks and bonds, but to them, too, the lucrative fields of personal finance are forbidden. So they, too, do not look favorably upon increases in the cost of money to them — that is to say, in the money they pay for your deposits.

Commercial banks in all their forms — National Banks, State Banks, Trust Companies — are permitted to play the field of finance. All types of lending are open to them, and they pick and choose whatever best serves their purposes at the time. Mortgage loans, personal loans, business loans, time loans, demand loans, collateralized loans, long term loans, short term loans — all fall within the scope of the commercial bank.

But while the commercial banks have the broadest lending powers, their ability to attract savings deposits has always been stilted by their inability to pay competitive interest rates on savings accounts. By regulation, they have been consistently kept to a maximum rate of about 1% less than that permitted savings banks. Reason: Back to the fundamental raison d' etre of savings accounts — to build homes; the government aims to discourage savings in banks whose essential function is not mortgaging.

The commercial banking industry has been repeatedly castigated by the guardians of low interest rates. Witness a forty page diatribe prepared for delivery in the House of Representatives by Representative Wright Patman, Democrat of Texas, in August, 1964: "If the bankers had been on the ball," Patman said in a key sentence, "if they had remained in the banking business and loaned money to people who needed it for houses, farms and other things — they would have enjoyed the billions of dollars worth of mortgage business that now goes to the savings and loan people."

Through the years, Representative Patman has been a respected champion of low interest rates, and has been a most effective voice in Congress for the savings bank and savings and loan industries as opposed to commercial banks. It is natural to sympathize with, and support his efforts to keep interest rates down for the protection of the potential home owner. It is in the public interest to have mortgage and loan rates kept low. But——

It is also in the public interest that the thrifty have their savings protected from erosion. Much more of the public is represented by depositors than by mortgagees and borrowers. Savings are of far greater importance to the public weal than borrowings. To decree against the welfare of the thrifty is tantamount to attacking old age and retirement.

The position represented by Representative Patman in favor of the homeowner would be defensible if the thrifty were not hurt by it. But, the thrifty's funds have suffered from inflation. Their savings plus the interest paid are together worth less today in purchasing power than when their savings were deposited. During the same time, the home buyer has profited materially from low interest mortgages. The value of his home has increased regularly at a rate beyond what he has paid in mortgage interest. In a non-inflationary era, the value would have shrunk through depreciation.

Yet these homes are made possible by the thrifty – who suffer for it. As a matter of fact, it's the thrifty who underwrite the nation's credit. Through banks and savings associations alone, depositors have supplied the credit-hungry populace with three hundred and thirty billion dollars. And its not enough. And it won't be enough. Everyone wants *today*, before we earn. We want cars and clothes, jewelry, television and vacations; we want new homes – all today, not tomorrow, even though we haven't even started to earn their cost yet. We mortgage our future to satisfy our desires today. We live in the utopia of borrow-now-pay-later. And we've been fortunate enough to pay later with dollars worth far less than when we borrowed them.

But not all of us have been smart enough to borrow dollars worth twelve loaves of bread and repay with dollars worth less than three loaves. Other millions have believed that savings rather than spending offers security for their twilight years. They've saved, and with inflation, watched their dreams of early retirement turn to dust. They've saved their dollars, each worth ten copies of the Sunday Times, and awakened to find they've been dreaming: the dollar buys only two copies.

They deserve better. The depositor deserves a return on his investment large enough, at the very least, to compensate for the effects of inflation.

In an open market, he could get it. Because money is now "tight" — it can be loaned out profitably and easily. And the "tight" money market comes at a time when commercial banks are undertaking an unprecedented expansion campaign. The banks find money hard to get at a time when they need *more* of it. In a free market it would mean you *would* get more for it.

But despite the constant cry for a free market, it in fact does not exist in banking. Regulations in favor of a comparatively small percentage of home and farm buyers have a stranglehold on savings deposit interest rates. And no prominent legislator has recognized the political potential of espousing the cause of the hundred million thrifty who have seen their lives' savings dissipated by twenty years of steady inflation. The government won't let banks pay their depositors *more*.

What's to be done?

One way is to organize. But that takes time, money, effort. We hope such an organization will come into being.

But in the meantime, there are ways to make your money multiply *legally* within the framework of the severe government restrictions. They are described in the section that follows.

PART II:

HOW TO GET 8% A YEAR ON YOUR SAVINGS – OR MORE

An overwhelming number of depositors are unaware of, if not indifferent to, the various avenues open to them to increase the earnings on their savings, despite the fact that banks and savings and loan associations have advertised and promoted these opportunities for years. It is surprising how few depositors have taken advantage of these offerings.

We have decided to act in the interest of all depositors and divulge, *in complete detail,* those proven methods of increasing income on savings *to a maximum.* To profit most from the information, it is important that the following pages be read with care and understood thoroughly.

CHAPTER 8

Multiply Your Money

Although as of this writing, no bank or S&L offers more than 5% on regular savings acccounts and up to 7½% on long-term certificates of deposit of $100,000, some depositors have been *and are* earning a net of 8% on their savings (and sometimes going up as high as 9½% – and 14¼% on short-term money.)

They do only what the banks and S&Ls openly permit. They follow the advertised and promoted offerings of the financial institutions to the letter. They gain their end of highest possible return on savings with maximum security by taking advantage only of what banks and S&Ls offer publicly. They use procedures which have been permissible for years and have the approval of the Federal Reserve, the FDIC, the Federal Home Loan Bank or the FSLIC.

Inflation has so eroded the value of the dollar that even at 8%, which is taxable as income, the thrifty are barely able to maintain the real value of their savings. But let's take 8% as a target minimum and see if the banks can afford it.

Conventional private home mortgages at their current rates of 7% to 9%, even adding the points charged, hardly make it possible to allow depositors a return of 8%. But the areas of personal financing do. For example, "small loans," and car and home improvement loans, usually yield 12% to 18% to the banks. Furthermore, the credit card field yields an unbelievably high percentage return on invested capital. Even figuring conservatively, the gross yield should exceed 24%. After deducting all costs of operations and losses from this gross figure, there is more than ample room left for an 8% or higher yield to depositors — the depositors who have provided the funds for the credit card operation.

It is not unusual for personal finance companies and commercial factors to pay interest to people who provide them with funds (usually in the form of debenture bonds) at rates of 8% and up. Compared to finance companies and commercial factors, banks can operate on a larger scale, gain a larger gross yield, operate at lower unit cost and suffer less bad debt loss. If finance companies are able to pay their sources of money 8% and more, banks should be able to equal or better that yield to depositors.

Offerings of both commercial banks *and* S&Ls *have* permitted some astute depositors to earn 8% or more. Mutual savings bank offerings have not done so in the past, but their advertisements since July 1968 indicate that some of their offerings lend themselves to use for increasing interest earnings well above the 5% level. We have seen that savings banks pay more than 8% for the smallest accounts. Yes, the banks *can* afford 8%.

But Federal Reserve (and other regulatory agencies) set a rate ceiling of 5% on regular savings accounts. What would happen if more than just the few who are now earning at least 8% were to learn how to legally circumvent government regulations? What troubles should we anticipate? What repercussions will there be to the public exposure of ways of earning up to 8% or more on savings, with federal insurance safety?

There are two major possibilities: First, many people would start earning considerably more on their savings, so that even with inflation and taxes on earnings, the real value of their nest eggs would not be eroded away. Second, either the banks or the regulatory agencies, or both acting in concert, would close the doors to the thrifty and prevent them from earning anything more than the decreed 5%.

If the great body of depositors are shown the ways to earn more on their savings safely, the disclosures will have been worthwhile. But if, by disclosing the ways, the means are closed, disclosure will have been self-defeating. What are the chances of either banks or federal agencies moving to prevent depositors from earning a better return? *Should* they so move? Would such moves on their part be in their own interest, or in the public interest? If called to task by a host of depositors, could the regulatory agencies justify such moves?

What banks and regulatory agencies *will* do is a question beyond our powers to answer. What they *should* do needs examination.

We start with one premise that we believe has been well established both in the preceding pages and by simple arithmetic: *The depositor is and has been entitled to a better return on his savings.* To recapitulate, while both business and labor have made great strides in increasing their return for their contribution to our society, the thrifty have seen the real value of their savings deteriorate to a small percentage of its original worth. The thrifty represent one of the largest segments of our society. The FDIC insures about one hundred million accounts, the FSLIC about half that number. There are more people who bank savings than belong to all of organized labor. There are more people with savings accounts than have stock holdings in corporations. There are more savings depositors than all the mortgages supplied by banks and insurance companies put together. What is in the interest of the thrifty is in the public interest. The regulatory agencies should *not* move against the depositors.

These agencies have either permitted or specifically approved all of the features of all of the types of accounts that make the high earnings practical. All of the features have been available to depositors for years. They have made no move to stop depositors from exploiting these accounts. Would these agencies have permitted, or approved, the salient features without knowing how they can be used? We think not. These agencies are, or should be, staffed by the most astute people in banking and finance. However, if the profitable use of these accounts were meant for just the few who are using them now, and not the general public, the practice is in grave jeopardy of being stopped. We must remember that Federal Reserve and the FDIC have insisted on the nominal ceiling of 5%. So how could they now justify 8%? We don't know the answer. All we can do is hope that the regulatory agencies will lift the interest ceilings to a rate high enough to offset inflation and pay a reasonable return on the invested sums.

It has been asked how we can reconcile our condemnation of inflation yet at the same time advocate inflationary higher interest rates. With every segment of our society having but the one concern — what's in it for me? — the thrifty, too, must act in their own self interest, at least temporarily. Until depositors are organized to stop inflation, their only hope of preserving the value of their savings is in higher interest rates.

The thrifty of this country have a definite course of action to follow. Until they're able to organize to foster their common interest, they should take advantage of every device offered by the banking industry to increase the income on their savings to the highest possible extent — as close to 8% as they can come. You can accomplish this with very little effort, provided the consortium of banks and government agencies does not move to forestall your actions. All details are completely described in the following chapters. They tell you how to multiply your money.

CHAPTER 9

Interest Earnings--Your Basic Tool for Greater Returns

To learn to take full advantage of banks' offerings, it is necessary to understand the use of money as a commodity. Bankers view money as the commodity it is; few of the thrifty do. Bankers almost invariably realize a high return; the thrifty seldom do. To understand money as a commodity, you should begin with an understanding of interest rates.

As a start, we will describe methods of computing interest, explain the difference between simple and compound interest, discuss the advantages of frequent compounding, and present tables from which interest information can be determined.

When a depositor places funds in a savings institution, he anticipates that his investment will grow with time. The extent to which his original deposit increases without additions by him is commonly called interest and represents to him the "profit" on his investment. This "profit" is calculated as a certain percent of his investment for a specific period or periods of time, usually per year.

Generally speaking, there are two types of interest: simple interest and compound interest. Let us examine the earning power of each form of interest upon the same principal.

Simple Interest

Assume that 5% simple interest per annum is to be paid on a principal of $10,000 held for one year. The interest, payable at the end of the first year, would be calculated as follows:

Interest = Principal x Rate x Time (in years) or

I = P x R x T

I = $10,000 x .05 x 1

I = $500

(Note that Rate of 5% is expressed as a decimal, .05, in the equation.)

If the $10,000 principal were held for two years at 5% simple interest, the interest earned at the end of two years would be calculated as follows:

I = P x R x T

I = $10,000 x .05 x 2

I = $1,000 at the end of two years

However, it should be noted that if the simple interest was paid to the depositor at the end of the first year and this $500 interest payment was deposited at 5% interest at the beginning of the second year, the interest earned by the end of the second year on this $500 amount (which was paid as interest but became a new principal after payment) would be $25. Thus, adding this $25 interest to the $1,000 interest earned on the original $10,000 principal gives a total interest of $1,025.

Compound Interest

When interest is added to the principal periodically, and this sum is used as the principal for the following time period, and this procedure is repeated for a certain number of periods, the final amount is called the compound amount. The difference between the original principal and the compound amount is called the compound interest.

Assume that 5% interest compounded annually is to be paid on a principal of $10,000. At the end of one year, the compound amount would be calculated as follows:

Accumulations on $1 = $(1 + i)^n$

where i is the interest rate for one compounding period (expressed as a decimal)

and n is the number of compounding periods to be included in the calculations.

(In this example the compounding period is annual and the interest rate is 5% per annum. Therefore i = .05. Since the time considered in this example is one year, or one compounding period, n = 1.)

Compound Amount = Principal x Accumulations on $1 or

$S = P \times (1+i)^n$

$S = \$10,000 \times (1 + .05)^1$

$S = \$10,000 \times 1.05$

$S = \$10,500$

and the interest earned is:

Compound Interest = Compound Amount — Original Principal or

$I = S - P$

$I = \$10,500 - \$10,000$

$I = \$500$

Note that this interest is exactly the same as the amount earned as simple interest after one year.

During the second year, $10,500 becomes the new principal.

Then

$S = \$10,500 \times 1.05$

$S = \$11,025$ at the end of the second year

and

$I = \$11,025 - \$10,000$

$I = \$1,025$ at the end of two years

Thus, compounding produced $25 more interest or "profit" than did simple interest over the same period of time, because the interest paid in the first year was automatically reinvested or redeposited. The same result was obtained with the simple interest example by converting the first year's interest to principal and depositing this sum at 5% for the second year.

Note that compound amount and compound interest can be calculated by applying the formula:

Compound Amount = Principal x (Accumulations on \$1)^n or

$S = P (1 + i)^n$

$S = \$10,000 (1 + .05)^2$

$S = \$10,000 (1.05) (1.05) = \$10,000 (1.1025)$

$S = \$11,025$

and

$I = \$11,025 - \$10,000$

$I = \$1,025$

Compound interest periods, also called conversion periods, may be other than annual. In such instances it is customary to quote a nominal annual rate of interest and then to stipulate the **number of compounding periods per year.** Thus, interest at

5% Compounded semi-annually =

2½% compounded each 6 months = .025

5% Compounded quarterly =

1¼% compounded each 3 months = .0125

5% Compounded monthly =

5/12% compounded each month = .0041667

5% Compounded daily =

5/365% compounded each day = .0001369863

Reference will be made to the following symbols in our further discussions of compound interest:

P = the original principal

S = the compound amount of P

m = the number of conversion periods per year

t = the time in years

n = the number of interest or conversion periods involved. (n = m x t)

j = the yearly interest rate (nominal rate) which is to be converted m times per year.

i = the interest rate per conversion period

$i = \dfrac{j}{m}$

$(1 + i)^n$ = the accumulation factor

r = the effective yearly rate of interest

I = the compound interest

When interest is compounded more frequently than once each year, the formula for computing the compound amount becomes:

$$S = P (1 + \tfrac{j}{m})^n$$

and the formula for compound interest is:

$$I = P[(1 + \tfrac{j}{m})^n - 1]$$

The yearly effective rate r corresponding to a given nominal rate j converted m times per year is the total amount of interest earned per year for each unit of principal greater than the nominal rate and can be found by employing the formula

$$r = [(1 + \tfrac{j}{m})^m - 1]$$

Examples:

1. To compute the total compound interest (I) earned on a principal of \$5,000 (P), deposited for a period of 5 years (t), at 5% (.05) interest (j), compounded daily (m):

   P = \$5,000

   j = .05

   m = 365

   j/m = .05/365 = .0001369863

   n = 365 x 5 yrs. = 1825

   $I = \$5,000 [(1 + .0001369863)^{1825} - 1]$

   This equation is readily solvable through the use of logarithms, tables of which are available in most libraries.

2. Of greater interest is computing the effective yearly rate (r) in the preceding example

   $r = [(1 + .0001369863)^{365} - 1]$

As shown in the table on page 98, r = 5.13%. This table shows the amount to which \$10,000 principal will accumulate in one year at 5% nominal rate converted with different frequencies.

The phrase "the magic of compound interest" is often seen and heard. We have compared a deposit at 5% simple interest paid annually with the same deposit at 5% compounded

Nominal Rate of Interest	J	5%	5%	5%	5%
Compounded		Annually	Semi-annually	Quarterly	Daily
No. of yearly Conversions	m	1	2	4	365
Rate of interest per period	$\frac{j}{m}$	5% .05	2½% .025	1¼% .0125	5/365% .0001369863
Effective Rate of Interest	r	5%	5.06%	5.09%	5.13%
Compound Amount on $10,000 held for one year	S	$10,500	$10,506	$10,509	$10,513
Total Interest for 1 year	I	$500	$506	$509	$513

annually. We found that the interest earned in both examples is the same if the simple interest, when paid, is deposited at the same rate of interest.

Likewise, 5% paid quarterly and 5% compounded quarterly yield the same results if interest is redeposited. In such cases the only real difference is that in the former case the depositor automatically receives interest on interest payment dates, and must himself deposit this interest to achieve the same results as with automatically compounded interest.

Thus, compound interest can be considered a convenient form of enforced saving. Conversely, people who use the income on their investments to meet their living expenses will find it more convenient to have the interest paid directly to them rather than compounded.

In recent years some variations of usual compound interest, which offer some advantage to the depositor, have been offered by some institutions. One type is more frequent compounding than payment of interest. An example is 5% interest, compounded daily and paid quarterly. As the table shows, on a $10,000 deposit compounded daily for a year, the yield is $513 compared to a $509 yield when compounded quarterly.

Savings institutions usually divide interest earning periods on deposits into quarters of the year. Thus, if quarters begin January 1, April 1, July 1, and October 1, deposits between these dates do not draw interest until the following quarterly period begins, and withdrawals between these dates receive interest only up to the end of the preceding quarter. Therefore, if interest earning periods are quarterly, a deposit of February 8th withdrawn July 12th would have earned interest only from April 1, through June 30, *unless the institution pays interest from date of deposit and to date of withdrawal.* If such savings institution credits funds received by the 10th of the month with interest from the first, known as 10 grace days, and a deposit is made by the 10th of the first month of the quarter, the investor in effect gains interest for the entire quarter. On a principal of $10,000 at 5% compounded quarterly, this would amount to a yield of $125 for the first quarter. If the ten grace days were not given, but interest were paid from date of deposit, the interest yield for the quarter would be $14 less, or $111 instead of $125, since interest is earned for ten days less than the full quarter.

Table I is designed to help the depositor make the computations and comparisons necessary to help him decide which of the many interest plans offered is most advantageous for him.

All computations were made using the formulae printed above together with seven place logarithm tables. Figures contained in these tables may vary from amounts actually paid by savings institutions by inconsequentially small amounts. Such variation would probably not exceed one twenty-fifth of 1% or .00025.

Table 1 shows the amount to which a $10,000 principal will accumulate at the end of each successive year up to fifteen (15) at a 5% nominal rate of interest when

    (a) It is compounded daily with interest retained

    (b) It is compounded quarterly with interest retained

    (c) It is compounded annually with interest retained.

This table also shows the average interest rate at the end of each year.

Table I may also be used to compute the compound amount at 5% compounded daily, quarterly or annually on any principal other than $10,000.

For a principal of $100,000 (10 x $10,000), simply multiply the amount printed in the table by 10; while for a principal of $1,000, divide the printed figure by 10; for $100 divide by 100; for $10, divide by 1,000.

Likewise, for a principal of $20,000 (2 x $10,000), multiply by 2; while for a principal of $5,000 (½ x $10,000), divide by 2.

For odd principals this table is readily usable as demonstrated by the following:

TABLE I

At the End of Year	Compound Amount on $10,000 Compounded Daily	Average Interest Per Year in %	Compound Amount on $10,000 Compounded Quarterly	Average Interest Per Year in %	Compound Amount on $10,000 Compounded Annually	Average Interest Per Year in %
1	10,513	5.13	10,509	5.09	10,500	5.00
2	11,052	5.26	11,045	5.23	11,025	5.13
3	11,619	5.40	11,608	5.36	11,576	5.25
4	12,214	5.54	12,199	5.50	12,155	5.39
5	12,841	5.68	12,820	5.64	12,763	5.53
6	13,499	5.83	13,474	5.79	13,401	5.66
7	14,192	5.99	14,160	5.94	14,071	5.82
8	14,919	6.15	14,881	6.10	14,775	5.97
9	15,684	6.32	15,639	6.27	15,513	6.11
10	16,488	6.49	16,436	6.44	16,289	6.29
11	17,334	6.67	17,274	6.61	17,103	6.46
12	18,223	6.85	18,154	6.80	17,959	6.63
13	19,157	7.04	19,078	6.98	18,856	6.81
14	20,139	7.24	20,050	7.18	19,799	7.00
15	21,172	7.45	21,072	7.38	20,789	7.19

For example: if an original principal is $4,573, to determine the compound amount at the end of five (5) years when 5% interest is compounded daily, note the figure in the first column next to the year 5. It is $12,841 for a $10,000 original principal.

We can obtain the correct result by multiplying $12,841 by .4573, which equals $5,871,1893 or $5,871.19.

To determine the compound amount on an original principal of $4,573 at the end of five (5) years when 5% interest is compounded quarterly, note the figure in the second compound amount column on a line with year 5. It is $12,820 for a $10,000 original principal. The result is obtained by multiplying $12,820 by .4573, which equals $5,862.5860 or $5,862.59. Therefore, at the end of 5 years a $4,573 original principal, when compounded quarterly with interest retained, will grow to $5,862.59 by the end of the fifth year. By comparison, daily compounding yielded $5,872.19 — not much difference.

This table may also be used to make some important observations from which useful conclusions can be drawn. For example, we often see newspaper advertisement in which we are invited to purchase a Savings Certificate or Bond which in ten years will yield 6.50% average annual interest. If we examine the second column in Table I showing the average interest rate at the end of each year when 5% interest on a principal is compounded daily and retained, we note that at the end of ten years the average interest rate is 6.49% which, rounded off becomes 6.5%. In fact, whenever 5% interest on a principal is compounded daily for ten years and all interest is accumulated in the account, the average interest rate will come to 6.5%. This is a fact — not a bargain. However, this kind of deposit has very real merit for people who have considerable funds which are not needed day to day and can, therefore, remain invested. Let us see why.

Historically, interest rates go up and down. About ten years ago they were 2¾% or 3%. Until mid-January of 1970, the interest rate offered was 5%. Today, up to 5¾% is available — and up to 7½% if one happens to be blessed with $100,000 in cash. In the near future, interest rates probably will not drop, but for the more distant future no one can predict. Should history repeat itself, they could drop. Twenty years ago, interest rates were as low as 1½%.

During the past couple of years, depositors for the first time have had an opportunity to insure for themselves an interest rate for a prolonged period of time. Unfortunately, many savings institutions, including Savings Banks and Savings and Loan Associations, cannot offer a guaranteed interest rate for any given period of time in the future, except for the recently permitted certificates for a maximum of two years. Except for these certificates, they can only state their current interest rate and/or an anticipated interest rate which is not even guaranteed for the coming quarter. However, commercial banks, in their quest for the depositor's dollar, have found that *they can* guarantee interest rates for long periods of time. This they do in the form of *bonds* currently with guaranteed interest rates up to 15 years. To make this type of deposit more attractive, some are offering that funds can be withdrawn at any quarterly anniversary of the deposit without penalty or loss of interest. The advantage that this combination offers to the long-term depositor is very great. Should interest rates rise in the future, the depositor is free to withdraw his deposit on that quarterly anniversary and make a deposit into a higher interest bearing account if any such is available. On the other hand, should interest rates drop, he is still guaranteed the high interest rate current at the time of his initial deposit.

Table II shows the amount to which a $10,000 principal will accumulate at the end of each successive year up to five (5) at nominal rates of interest between 4% and 5½% in 1/10% gradations when compounded annually, quarterly, and daily with interest accumulated in each case respectively.

Table II may also be used to compute the compound amount at the end of one to five years, for *any* interest rate between 4% and 5½% compounded daily, quarterly or annually on *any* principal other than $10,000.

TABLE II

COMPOUNDED ANNUALLY

At the end of year	4%	4.1%	4.2%	4.3%	4.4%	4.5%	4.6%	4.7%
1	10,400	10,410	10,420	10,430	10,440	10,450	10,460	10,470
2	10,816	10,837	10,857	10,878	10,899	10,920	10,941	10,962
3	11,248	11,281	11,313	11,346	11,379	11,412	11,444	11,477
4	11,699	11,744	11,789	11,834	11,880	11,925	11,971	12,017
5	12,167	12,225	12,284	12,343	12,402	12,462	12,522	12,582

COMPOUNDED QUARTERLY

At the end of year	4%	4.1%	4.2%	4.3%	4.4%	4.5%	4.6%	4.7%
1	10,406	10,416	10,427	10,437	10,448	10,458	10,468	10,478
2	10,829	10,850	10,872	10,893	10,915	10,936	10,958	10,980
3	11,268	11,302	11,335	11,369	11,403	11,437	11,471	11,505
4	11,726	11,772	11,819	11,866	11,913	11,960	12,008	12,055
5	12,202	12,262	12,323	12,384	12,446	12,508	12,570	12,632

COMPOUNDED DAILY

At the end of year	4.8%	4.9%	5%	5.1%	5.2%	5.3%	5.4%	5.5%
1	10,408	10,418	10,428	10,439	10,449	10,459	10,470	10,481
2	10,831	10,853	10,875	10,897	110,919	10,941	10,963	10,985
3	11,272	11,307	11,341	11,375	11,410	11,444	11,479	11,514
4	11,732	11,779	11,827	11,875	11,923	11,971	12,019	12,067
5	12,209	12,271	12,333	12,395	12,458	12,521	12,584	12,648

COMPOUNDED ANNUALLY

At the end of year	4.8%	4.9%	5%	5.1%	5.2%	5.3%	5.4%	5.5%
1	10,480	10,490	10,500	10,510	10,520	10,530	10,540	10,550
2	10,983	11,004	11,025	11,046	11,067	11,088	11,109	11,130
3	11,510	11,543	11,576	11,609	11,643	11,676	11,709	11,742
4	12,063	12,109	12,155	12,201	12,248	12,295	12,341	12,388
5	12,642	12,702	12,763	12,824	12,885	12,946	13,008	13,070

At the end of year	4.8%	4.9%	5%	5.1%	5.2%	5.3%	5.4%	5.5%
COMPOUNDED QUARTERLY								
1	10,489	10,499	10,509	10,520	10,530	10,541	10,551	10,561
2	11,001	11,023	11,045	11,067	11,089	11,110	11,132	11,154
3	11,539	11,573	11,608	11,642	11,677	11,711	11,746	11,781
4	12,103	12,151	12,199	12,247	12,296	12,344	12,393	12,442
5	12,694	12,757	12,820	12,884	12,948	13,012	13,076	13,141
COMPOUNDED DAILY								
1	10,492	10,502	10,513	10,523	10,534	10,545	10,555	10,566
2	11,007	11,029	11,052	11,074	11,097	11,119	11,141	11,164
3	11,548	11,583	11,619	11,654	11,689	11,725	11,760	11,796
4	12,116	12,165	12,214	12,263	12,313	12,363	12,413	12,463
5	12,712	12,777	12,841	12,906	12,971	13,036	13,102	13,169

As when using Table I, for a principal of $100,000, multiply the amount printed in the table by 10; for a principal of $1,000 divide by 10; for a principal of $20,000, multiply by 2; while for a principal of $5,000, divide by 2 (or multiply by 0.5). Likewise, for an odd principal like $13,246, multiply by 1.3246; for $2,345, multiply by 0.2345.

For interest rates between 4% and 5½% in gradations of other than 1/10% (for example: 5¼% or 5.25%) simple interpolation is required to obtain the compound amount.

Table III lists the effective yield for various nominal interest rates when compounded annually, quarterly and daily.

Table III Effective Annual Rate

Nominal Rate	Compounded		
	Annually	Quarterly	Daily
4. %	4.00%	4.06%	4.08%
4.1	4.10	4.16	4.18
4.2	4.20	4.27	4.28
4.3	4.30	4.37	4.39
4.4	4.40	4.48	4.49
4.5	4.50	4.58	4.59
4.6	4.60	4.68	4.70
4.7	4.70	4.78	4.81
4.8	4.80	4.89	4.92
4.9	4.90	4.99	5.02
5.0	5.00	5.09	5.13
5.1	5.10	5.20	5.23
5.2	5.20	5.30	5.34
5.3	5.30	5.41	5.45
5.4	5.40	5.51	5.55
5.5	5.50	5.61	5.66

CHAPTER 10

Daily Interest Pays More

Now that you know how to use interest rates, let's apply your knowledge to an examination of bank lending practices.

Whenever anyone borrows money, be it from bank, money lender or shylock, he pays interest on the money from the moment he borrows it. When banks quote an interest rate to a borrower, that rate is usually for a 360 day year, not a 365 day year. If the money is kept for a full 365 day year, a 6% rate actually becomes an annual rate of 6.0833%. If the borrower pays the interest *at the end* of each quarter, the effective annual rate is 6.2%. If the interest on a (365 day) year loan is deducted in advance, and the rate is 6% based on a 360 day year, the effective annual rate is 6½%, provided that the loan is paid off in one lump sum at the *end* of the year. However, with this same loan, if the interest is all deducted in advance, and the borrower is required to repay the loan in 12 equal monthly installments, the actual effective annual interest rate is 12-2/3%. (If the 6% rate is for a full 365 day year, the effective rate is 12½%.)

The new Truth-in-Lending Law now requires banks and other lenders to state the actual effective annual interest rate. Heretofore, personal loans requiring monthly repayment were advertised as 6% loans, and the unwitting borrower paid a true interest rate of more than 12%.

Under any circumstances, banks and other lenders always charge the borrower for at least every day the borrower has the money. However, this is not so when banks borrow money from you. Again, one must remember that depositing in a bank is lending money to the bank. Most banks take your money, but should you withdraw it prior to their interest-paying date, you will earn nothing. If one deposits a sum in an institution that pays interest semi-annually, then withdraws the funds even a week prior to the half year period, his interest is zero. The person who deposits a monthly pay check and then gradually withdraws funds for living expenses, gives the bank the use of his money for many days or weeks each month, but earns nothing for his magnanimity. That is, unless the bank pays daily interest (interest from date of deposit to date of withdrawal).

Daily Interest

By federal regulation, commercial banks have not been permitted to pay interest rates on regular savings accounts that could compete with the rates permitted to be paid by savings banks and savings and loan associations. Because their interest rates were forced to be lower, the commercial banks had to find some way to attract savings deposits that would normally be placed in the conventional savings institutions. Some six years ago, a number of banks, including such giants as Chase Manhattan and First National City, hit upon the idea of paying their savings depositors interest from date of deposit to date of withdrawal. This meant that money on deposit one day earned one day's interest — just as a bank charges a borrower per day. This also meant that a deposited paycheck, from which withdrawals were made to meet living expenses, earned interest on each dollar on deposit for each day it remained on deposit. Even though the interest rate was lower, many people learned that the lower rate earned them far more interest than the higher rate paid by savings banks. But six years ago, money was not tight, and some banks, including First National City dropped the idea after a short trial. Apparently the cost of record keeping of daily interest on small amounts made the practice unprofitable. But Chase Manhattan and some others stuck to their guns and continued to offer and promote daily interest paying accounts. Gradually, savings and loan associations followed suit so that today many commerical banks, now again including First National City, and savings and loan associations not only offer, but aggressively promote their daily interest bearing savings accounts. But true to form, the mutual savings banks of New York State, not to speak of other areas, didn't budge until July, 1968 when they finally followed suit. Many commercial banks and S&Ls have paid interest from date of deposit to date of withdrawal, savings banks only recently did. Apparently they were so sure that the mass of people automatically gave them their money, that they had not felt compelled to offer what their competition did. Ironically, savings banks spend millions on advertising to promote the concept that they are "peoples' banks." But not until recently did it occur to them that the "people" might want to be paid for the daily use of their money just as they were being paid by commercial banks and S&Ls.

What is important is that probably for the first time in recent banking history, many banks have acted upon the fact that depositors *lend* them money and should be paid for doing so. This may seem a small concession from bankers, but it is one of the key features to greatly increase one's income on savings. In addition, of course, people can earn interest on money they regularly spend — from the day they receive it to the day they spend it. And, for the record, it should be noted that the practice of paying daily interest has existed for six or more years, and is not in violation of Federal Reserve Board, FDIC, Federal Home Loan Bank or FSLIC regulations.

No depositor need fear that he is cheating a bank or S&L if he takes full advantage of daily interest, even if he withdraws most of the money shortly after opening the account. The banks and S&Ls that offer it are anxious to obtain these deposits, even for only a few days, as the following excerpts from their advertisements clearly indicate.

Says First National City Bank in New York, the nation's second largest bank:

"You won't lose any interest in a Passbook Savings Account at First National City. That's because we pay you interest every day your money is on deposit.

"This isn't the case at many financial institutions.

"You see, with some savings accounts, if you make a withdrawal before the end of the calendar quarter — you lose interest on that money from the beginning of the quarter.

"But First National City pays 4% interest per year, and we pay interest at this rate from day of deposit to day of withdrawal. What this adds up to is a savings account with complete flexibility. One that lets you make withdrawals at any time, without losing a penny's worth of interest providing the account remains open . . . "

The Chase Manhattan Bank, N.A., granddaddy of daily interest to date of withdrawal, offers the same features, as do many other commercial banks. With their hundreds of offices, and free banking by mail (postage-paid envelopes are provided), these accounts are readily available to anyone in the U.S.A.

And now finally in New York City, as savings and loans in other parts of the country do, West Side Federal S&L is able to go the banks one better. They advertise:

"New in N.Y.C. and ONLY at West Side Federal 'day of deposit day of withdrawal' savings accounts at 5% per annum compounded quarterly, the highest rate in the country . . .

"No notice required for withdrawals . . .

"Earn from day in to day out. Every day your funds are in they earn — as long as a balance of $1 remains at the end of the quarter.

"10 bonus days every month. Money deposited up to the 10th of any month earns full dividends from the 1st — providing the deposit remains to the end of the quarter . . .   .

" 'Stock market in-and-outers' need a 'day of deposit day of withdrawal savings account' . . . "

The following pages contain reprints of ads soliciting savings accounts that pay interest from day in to day out. As of July 1, 1968, several New York Savings Banks began offering 4¾% interest on these accounts, but without the 10 grace days each month.

It is important not to confuse "interest to date of withdrawal" with "interest to date of withdrawal provided funds have remained on deposit for three (or six) months." The former, true daily interest, is of much greater value to the depositor seeking the greatest return than is the latter.

The 5% daily interest plus the value of 10 bonus days every month as offered by some savings and loan associations is far more valuable than the 4% or 4¾% without bonus days offered by commercial banks and some savings banks. However, in the use of these accounts to multiply earnings, convenience plus 4% or 4¾% may be better than inconvenience and 5%. If enough people will let their local banks and savings and loan associations know that accounts will be opened therein only if daily interest to date of withdrawal is paid, perhaps many more will adopt this policy. Remember that First National City reinstituted daily interest, undoubtedly because they found it to their advantage to do so. Enough requests may bring much of the industry into line.

Understanding daily interest is but a step on the road to higher return on one's savings. Another step is the gaining of an awareness of "bonus" or "grace" days, then the interrelationship between the two.

Most savings institutions offer some form of bonus or grace days. Most common is: deposits received by the 10th day of January, April, July or October will earn interest from the first of that month. Less common, but quite prevalent in the savings and loan industry, is: money deposited up to the 10th of any

Figure 15. Fidelity Federal Savings and Loan Advertisement.

THE GREENWICH SAVINGS BANK

5% a year
ON REGULAR SAVINGS ACCOUNTS

Latest dividend declared
Dividends paid from Day of Deposit
Compounded Quarterly

Money deposited by **JULY 10**
earns dividends from **JULY 1**

Your money doubles in 14 years when compounded quarterly at 5% a year. Your deposit at the end of 14 years would have an average yearly growth of 7.18%. While future dividend rates cannot be guaranteed, The Greenwich has paid uninterrupted dividends since 1833.

5% a year

TIME DEPOSIT ACCOUNTS

Recent legislation now permits The Greenwich Savings Bank to offer you a new and attractive service, a time deposit account with a guaranteed interest rate of 5% a year, compounded quarterly. Maturities may range from 6 months to 2 years—minimum account $500—maximum $25,000. For complete and detailed information please mail the coupon below.

DAY OF DEPOSIT TO DAY OF WITHDRAWAL ACCOUNTS

In addition to Regular Savings Accounts and Time Deposit Accounts the bank will have available, on and after July 1, 1968, special accounts which will pay dividends from day of deposit to day of withdrawal, provided a minimum balance remains in the account until the end of the dividend period. It is anticipated that in the quarter beginning July 1, 1968, the dividend rate on these special accounts will be 4¾% a year, compounded quarterly.

----- **SEND THIS COUPON** ----- T-7

The Greenwich Savings Bank, P.O. Box 11, Midtown Station
New York City 10018

I enclose $_____ . Please open a savings account in my name, as checked.

Individual Account
Joint Account with _____
Trust Account for _____

Check the office in which you wish to save:
☐ 36th St. ☐ Madison Ave. ☐ 57th St. ☐ 14th St. ☐ B'way-Cedar

Sign here _____
Print Name here _____
Address _____
City _____ State _____ Zip Code _____

☐ Please send me information about 5% a year Time Deposit account.
☐ Please send me information about Day of Deposit-Day of Withdrawal account.

Enclose with check or money order. Do not mail cash.

Broadway-Sixth Ave. at 36th St.
515 Madison Ave. at 53rd St.
3 West 57th St. near Fifth Ave.
101 West 14th St. at Sixth Ave.
120 Broadway at Cedar St.

ALL OFFICES OPEN
8:30 A.M. to 5:30 P.M.
Monday through Friday

36th Street Office also open
Monday and Thursday to 6:30 P.M.

Telephone LA 4-6000

Member Federal Deposit
Insurance Corporation

Figure 16. Greenwich Savings Bank Advertisement.

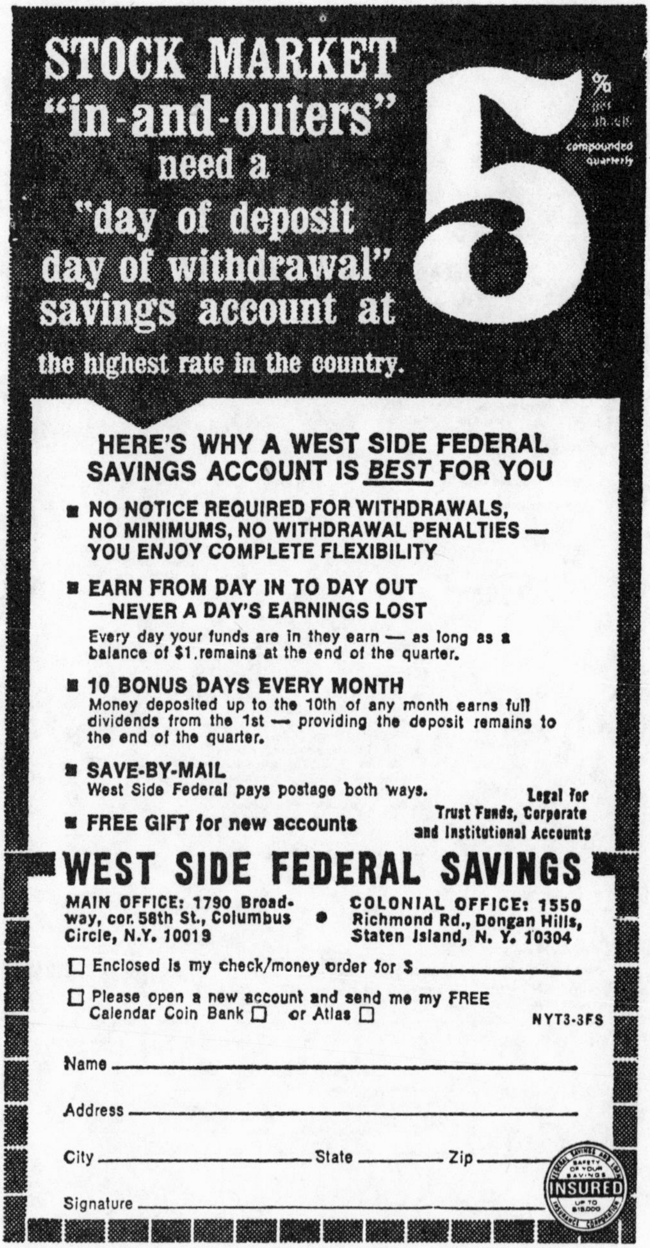

Figure 16A. West Side Federal Savings and Loan Advertisement.

What Rate Do You Want?
Your Choice!

$4\frac{1}{2}\%$ PASSBOOK WORKING FUND

Dividends compounded quarterly
Deposit by 20th earn from 1st of month
Withdrawals without notice

5% INVESTMENT CERTIFICATE

$2,000 minimum and multiples of $1,000
4½% compounded semi-annually plus ½% bonus after each year
Redeemable without notice

$5\frac{1}{4}\%$ CERTIFICATE OF DEPOSIT

Only $10,000 minimum
4½% compounded semi-annually plus ¾% bonus after each year
Redeemable without notice
Highest rate permitted by Federal regulations

Savings insured up to $15,000 by Federal Savings and Loan
Insurance Corporation, a permanent U.S. Government Agency

GREEN STAMPS WITH EACH DEPOSIT

Get one stamp for each $1.00 deposit up to 1,000 stamps and have
your choice of 2,500 nationally advertised gifts in
S & H Green Stamp Catalogue

MAIL CHECK TO:

WESTVIEW
FEDERAL SAVINGS
AND LOAN ASSOCIATION
Established 1922

1000 Ingleside Ave., Baltimore, Maryland 21228

FOR ADDITIONAL INFORMATION CALL COLLECT 301-747-6200
Check Enclosed $_____. Type: 4½% ☐, 5% ☐, 5¼% ☐
Account: Individual ☐, Joint ☐, Corporate ☐, Other _____
Passbook or Certificate and appropriate Signature Card will be mailed immediately

NAME _____ TAX I.D. NO. _____

ADDRESS _____

CITY_____STATE_____ ZIP _____

PLEASE SEND: ☐ PREPAID ADDRESSED ENVELOPES, ☐ S & H GREEN STAMPS,
☐ S & H GIFT CATALOGUE

Figure 17. Westview Federal Savings & Loan Advertisement

month earns full dividends from the 1st — providing the deposit remains to the end of the quarter. (See West Side Federal S&L ad reprint 1. Figure 16A, page 116.

In some states, as many as twenty grace days are permitted to be offered. Thus, Federal Savings and Loan Associations in Baltimore, Maryland offer, at the rate of 4½%, (recently increased to 4¾%) dividends from the first of any month on funds deposited up to the 20th of the month, as shown in Figure 17, page 117.

Again for the record, it should be noted that the practice of granting grace days has been in existence for many many years and is not in violation of any of the rules or regulations of the governmental regulatory agencies — even though it means that a bank is paying interest on money when it doesn't really have the money on deposit.

CHAPTER 11

Breaking the 5% Ceiling
Grace and Bonus Days

Actually, the granting of grace or bonus days is the first chink in the armor of the 5% interest rate ceiling — the allowance for banks to pay interest on non-existent money. The chink became a crack with the advent of daily interest, and the armor eventually fell apart, as will soon be demonstrated. But first it is necessary to understand the mechanics of exploiting daily interest and grace days to the advantage of the depositor. Although it is elementary, and the rewards for the effort involved may be small, it should nevertheless be understood throughly.

The first thing to remember is that once an account is opened, it should be kept open, even if with only the $1 or $5 minimum required. It is costly to the bank and time consuming to the depositor to open and close accounts.

To demonstrate several ways to increase interest earnings on savings accounts, various types of accounts will be used. In describing the features of each of these accounts, for brevity and clarity, abbreviations will be used as shown in the following:

> DD = Interest from *day* of *deposit* .
> DW = Interest to *day* of *withdrawal*

DD-DW = Interest from day of deposit to day of withdrawal (daily interest)
DQ = Interest compounded *daily,* paid *quarterly*
QQ = Interest compounded *quarterly,* paid *quarterly*
DD-DW/QQ = Daily interest compounded and paid quarterly

Note that 5% interest compounded quarterly (QQ) and left on deposit for a year, yields the same as 5.09% simple interest, while compounded daily (DQ) yields 5.13% simple interest. Since the entire difference in interest on a $1,000 deposit left for an entire year is only 40 cents, the advantage of daily compounding over quarterly compounding is insignificant, certainly when compared to the other opportunities to increase interest earnings to a meaningful degree.

Each of the following examples assumes that the depositor has $10,000 available (in addition to the $1 to $5 used to keep each account open). In practice, any sum, be it $1,000 or $15,000, can be used.

If $10,000 is deposited on October 1st into a commercial bank paying 4½% from day of deposit to day of withdrawal (DD-DW), with interest compounded and paid quarterly (QQ), by the end of December the interest earnings are $112.50. (As of mid-January 1970, most commercial banks raised interest rates on savings accounts from 4% to 4½%.)

If the same deposit were put into a savings bank paying 4¾% from day of deposit to day of withdrawal, compounded and paid quarterly (DD-DW/QQ), in the same period the interest earnings are $118.75.

An identical deposit made into a savings and loan association paying 5% (DD-DW/QQ) yields $125.

Example 1

(In this and the following examples, it is assumed that the various accounts to be used have balances of the minimum amount required, usually $1 to $5 in each account.)

Step 1   On Oct. 1, deposit $10,000 into a savings account (Acct No, 1) in a commercial bank paying 4½% DD-DW/QQ. (E.g.: Chase Manhattan, First National City, etc.)

Step 2   On Oct. 10, withdraw the $10,000 deposited in Step 1, walk around the corner, and deposit the $10,000 in a savings and loan association (Acct. No. 2) paying 5% DD-DW/QQ (or DQ) and offering 10 grace days at the beginning of each quarter, with interest payable three business days prior to the end of the quarter. (e.g.: West Side Federal S&L and New York & Suburban S&L in New York or Fidelity Federal S&L in California, etc.)

By the end of December, on the $10,000 you will collect $125 in interest from the S&L (Acct. No. 2) *plus* approximately $11 from the commercial bank (Acct. No. 1). Thus, the total yield for the three months is $136, which is equivalent to a 5.4% annual rate.

Step 3   On Dec. 29, three business days prior to the end of the quarter, withdraw the $10,000 plus $125 interest from the S & L (Acct. No. 2). Keep the $125 interest and deposit the $10,000 into the bank (Acct. No. 1), as you did in Step 1.

Step 4   On Jan. 9, withdraw the $10,000 from the bank (Acct. No. 1) and deposit same into the S & L (Acct. No. 2) as you did in Step 2.

Steps 3 & 4 accomplished the following: By the end of March, $125 was earned from the S & L (Acct. No. 2) plus over $13 from the bank (Acct. No. 1), to a total of more than $138. The yield is 5½%.

Step 5   Again, three business days prior to the end of the quarter, on March 27, repeat Step 3.

Step 6   On April 10, repeat Step 4.

By the end of June, Steps 5 and 6 resulted once again in

$125 interest earned from the S & L (Acct. No. 2), but this time over $17 was earned from the bank (Acct. No. 1) to a total of over $142, or an annual rate of 5.69%. If Steps 3 & 4 (or 5 & 6) are repeated on June and Sept. 26th and July and Oct. 10th respectively, the earnings for these succeeding quarters continues at the annual rate of 5.69%. To make it still more attractive, each time were the interest earned added to the $10,000, instead of being withdrawn, or, in other words, if the interest is permitted to compound, the annual rate of interest becomes 5.78%.

Example 1, using a 4½% daily interest bank account and a 5% daily interest savings and loan account, is only the first and most elementary, yet with eight transactions a year consisting of deposits and withdrawals, 5% is increased to over 5½%, or 5.09% is increased to 5¾%. The second, and still elementary example yields still higher interest.

Example 2

Step 1   On Oct. 1, deposit $10,000 into a savings account in a savings and loan association (Acct. No. 1) paying 5% DD-DW/QQ and giving 10 grace days at the start of each quarter with interest payable three business days prior to the end of the quarter.

Step 2   On Oct. 10, withdraw the $10,000 deposited in Step 1, and deposit it into an account in another S & L (Acct. No. 2) paying interest in exactly the same manner as the S & L used in Step 1.

By the end of December, the same $10,000 again will have earned $125 from Acct. No. 2, plus more than $12 from Acct. No. 1, to a total of over $137, or an annual interest rate of 5½%. (This compares to 5.4% for the same period in example 1.)

Step 3   On Dec. 29, three business days prior to the end of the quarter, withdraw the $10,000 and $125 interest from Acct. No. 2. Keep the $125 interest, and deposit the $10,000 into the first S & L (Acct. No. 1).

Step 4 On Jan. 9, withdraw the $10,000 from Acct. No. 1 and deposit same into Acct. No. 2, as you did in Step 2.

Steps 3 & 4 accomplished the following: By the end of March, $125 was earned from Acct. No. 2, plus over $15 from Acct. No. 1, to a total of more than $140, and a yield of 5.6% (as compared to 5½% in example 1).

Step 5 Again, three business days prior to the end of the quarter, on March 27, repeat Step 3.

Step 6 On April 10, repeat Step 4.

By the end of June, Steps 5 & 6 resulted in $125 interest earned from Acct. No. 2 plus over $19 from Acct. No. 1, to a total of over $144, or an annual rate of 5.77% (as compared to 5.69% in example 1). If this procedure is repeated on June 26th and July 10th, and again on Sept. 26th and Oct. 10th, the earnings for these successive quarters continues at the annual rate of 5.77%. Each time, were the interest earned permitted to compound instead of being withdrawn, the annual rate of interest becomes equivalent to over 5.85% (as compared to 5.7% in example 1).

Summarizing, $10,000 at 5% yields $500 in a year, or $509 if interest is compounded quarterly for the year. Example 1 shows that the $500 can be increased to about $560, and example 2 shows that this can be further increased to about $575, or $585 if interest is permitted to compound.

Example 3

This example yields the same results as does example 2, but with greater convenience. Simply replace Acct. No. 2 in example 2 with a second account in the same S & L as Acct. No. 1 is in. Thus, Acct. No. 1 may be in your name alone, while Acct. No. 2 can be a joint account. Follow the same procedure with Acct. No. 1 and Acct. No. 2 as was done in example 2, and the results will be the same, except that it is not necessary to visit two different S & Ls.

At this point it should be repeated that it is necessary to keep each account open with at least the minimum required, usually $1 to $5, since daily interest is only paid if an account remains open till the end of the quarter. ALWAYS KEEP A MINIMUM BALANCE IN EACH ACCOUNT, OR YOU MAY LOSE THE ADVANTAGES OF DAILY INTEREST.

CHAPTER 12

Short Term Deposits-- from 9½% to 14¼%

An interesting sidelight to the use of grace and bonus days is appropriate. Many institutions, particularly savings and loan associations, offer ten grace days at the beginning of each month, provided the funds remain in till the end of the quarter. This has been explained in the advertisements of the New York and California savings and loan associations described previously in this section. In addition, most pay interest for the quarter and honor withdrawals during the last three business days of each quarter.

When individuals, businesses, banks and even governmental agencies or authorities have large funds on hand for short periods of time, often thirty days or less, they resort to the purchase of short term obligations – U.S. Treasury Bills or commercial "paper" – rather than leave the money idle in checking accounts where it earns no interest. Interest rates on this short-term paper varies from day to day and according to dates of maturity. Government issues this paper to supply its day to day financing as compared to obligations for long terms which often entail higher and more steady interest rates. Every day tremendous sums of this paper are bought at lower than generally prevailing interest rates, as each day great sums reach maturity and are repaid. Recently, however, short-term paper rates have escalated so that yields of 8% are not uncommon.

Few of these short-term paper purchasers have availed themselves of the opportunity to gain higher rates and greater convenience and flexibility. Of course, when paper rates are below 5%, the savings and loans that offer 5% daily interest could be used without concern about maturity dates. But now let us look at the case of the short-term paper purchaser on March 10th, June 10th, September 10th or December 10th, and consider only those who can commit their funds for 16 or 17 days. Instead of purchasing paper that matures in 17 days, if $100,000 is deposited into one of the 5% daily interest S & Ls, a full month's interest of $417 is earned - a yield of 8.94% per annum. And if the $100,000 were available on June 10th and was needed on June 26th, for these 16 days, $417 would still be earned — *a yield at the rate of 9½%!* And it is simple to accomplish — by making use of grace and bonus days.

Choose any institution that gives interest from the first of any month on deposits received by the 10th, and that also pays interest and permits withdrawals during the last three business days of the quarter. Many, particularly S & Ls as previously described, offer these 10 grace days, and most offer the last three bonus days. It is not even necessary that the institution pay daily interest. $100,000 deposited on September 10th and withdrawn on the 26th will earn a full month's interest of approximately $417, even though the funds have been on deposit for only 16 days — and that's interest at an annual rate of 9½%!

Now, let us refer back to the advertisement of a typical S & L in Maryland, as reproduced on page 117. Note that the ad reads:

> "4½% Passbook Working Fund
> Dividends compounded quarterly
> Deposit by 20th earn from 1st of month
> Withdrawals without notice"*

Where 20 grace days are offered, even at the lower rate of 4¾% an even greater return is possible. Deposits made on the 20th of March, June, September or December earn a full month's interest by the end of that month. Even though daily

*Sometime prior to February 1970, this rate was increased to 4¾%.

interest is not paid, in just 10 or 11 days, on a $100,000 deposit, over $395 is earned as interest — *a yield at the rate of approx. 14¼%!*

And, as an added inducement, the same ad says:

> "Green Stamps With Each Deposit
> Get one stamp for each $1.00 deposit
> up to 1,000 stamps . . . ."

Depositors have reported to us that they have received one S & H stamp for each dollar deposited, to totals exceeding the 1,000 stamp limitation. (D.S. in Maryland reported 10,000 stamps for a $10,000 deposit; S.S. in New York claimed 23,000 stamps for deposits of $23,000.) So, why not add the value of the trading stamps (whatever that may be) to the *14¼%*? What banks won't do to lure the funds of the thrifty!

During the past several years, the savings and loan industry in various parts of the nation has broken new ground in offering more attractive packages of grace and bonus days. To meet this competition, the "peoples banks," the mutual savings banks of New York, belatedly have awakened.

For the quarter starting October 1st, 1969, the New York Bank for Savings announced what they call "three new dividend extras." (See Fig. 18, page 128.)

First, the bank now offers to pay interest (at 5% per annum) on funds withdrawn prior to the end of the quarter — but only to the first of the month in which such withdrawal is made. Thus, funds withdrawn on December 18th earn interest through December 1st, whereas heretofore, interest was lost for October and November. It's not daily interest, but it is an improvement over the previous policy of paying interest only if funds were kept in the bank through the end of the quarter.

Second, they now compound interest daily rather than quarterly. As was previously pointed out, the old 5% compounded quarterly was equivalent to 5.09% simple interest, while the new daily compounding brings the effective rate to

THREE NEW DIVIDEND EXTRAS
AT
THE NEW YORK BANK FOR SAVINGS
On Regular
Savings Accounts
Anticipated for the quarter starting October 1

5% A YEAR Dividends Monthly

Money withdrawn before end of quarter will earn dividends compounded daily to the 1st of the month in which withdrawal is made at the rate in effect the previous quarter, provided a minimum balance is maintained to end of quarter when dividends will be payable. Latest dividend 5% a year.

Dividends Compounded Daily

On both Regular Savings Accounts and Day of Deposit to Day of Withdrawal Accounts, your money now earns dividends compounded daily from day of deposit.

10 Extra Dividend Days Every Month

Money deposited by the 10th of ANY month earns dividends from the 1st of the month. Money deposited after the 10th earns dividends from Day of Deposit—dividends are payable at the end of the quarter.

One Passbook—and with it you can bank at all offices.

Fig. 18. Extra Bonus Days Offered by A New York Mutual Savings Bank

5.13%. That's an increase of four one hundredths of one percent. It makes good ad copy, but puts few pennies in the depositors' pockets.

Third, the bank offers "10 extra dividend days *every* month." "Money deposited by the 10th of ANY month earns dividends from the 1st of the month."

Note that there is no requirement that funds remain till the end of the quarter (as all the S & Ls except Coast Federal seem to require). An "extra" that is not mentioned in the ad, but is of importance to the depositor, is that interest is added and withdrawal may be made without loss three business days prior to the end of each quarter.

The combination of monthly dividends plus 10 grace days each month plus interest paid and withdrawals permitted three business days before the end of the quarter again offers the alert depositor the opportunity to earn sizeable extras.

As with the S & Ls (West Side Federal S & L, New York and Surburban Federal S & L and Fidelity Federal S & L), funds deposited on the 10th of March, June, September or December and withdrawn three business days prior to the end of the month in which the deposit was made will earn interest at the rate of approximately 9½%. In addition, at this bank, funds deposited on the 10th of the remaining eight months and withdrawn on the first of the month following the deposit will earn interest at an average rate of 7.1%

If the depositor keeps both a 4¾% daily interest account *and* one of these new 5% accounts, for a full year or for any full quarter he can earn a return equal to 6¾% interest. To accomplish this, on the 10th of any month deposit the funds into the 5% account.

(1) If the month of deposit is March, June, September or December, three business days before the end of the same month withdraw the funds (leaving a minimum balance) and deposit them into the 4¾% account.

(2) If the month of deposit is any of the remaining eight

months, on the first day of the month following the deposit in the 5% account, withdraw the funds (leaving a minimum balance) and deposit them into the 4¾% account.

(3) On the 10th of each month, withdraw the funds from the 4¾% account (leaving a minimum balance) and deposit them into the 5% account.

(4) Each month just repeat the procedure outlined in (1), (2) and (3).

As of October 1969, most of the "peoples banks" started offering the "10 extra dividend days every month," but few, if any, except the New York Bank for Savings offered the "5% a year dividends *monthly.*" It is the *combination* of the *10 extra days* plus *monthly dividends* that make the high returns described above possible.

At the savings banks that offer only the 10 extra dividend days every month (but not the dividends monthly), short term deposits can still earn an average of 9%, but only on deposits made on the 10th of March, June, September and December and withdrawn three business days prior to the end of that month.

CAUTION: Savings banks *may* require that *any* deposits made by *check* remain in the account for a full month before withdrawals can be made against them. Inquiry revealed that the New York Bank for Savings requires seven business days before withdrawals can be made against deposits by New York bank checks. Check your bank's clearance-time and withdrawal regulations beforehand — you may find your funds frozen for a month.

By mid 1968 something new was entered in the field of extras offered to the thrifty, an extra that tremendously increases short-term yields. The Coast Federal Savings & Loan Association in Los Angeles, one of the largest in the country, with assets in excess of three quarters of a billion dollars, has been regularly advertising in the New York Times with the not-unusual offer of 5% compounded daily (and paid semi-annually). What *is* most unusual is their statement that "all funds received by the 10th earn from the first, thereafter from date of deposit" and "earnings paid to date of withdrawal *with no minimum qualifying period necessary!*" (emphasis added)

At first glance this offer appears to be no great shakes. But Coast Federal has omitted a clause that others include, and therein lies the attractive monetary opportunity for the alert depositor. Other banks and S & Ls offer earnings from the first on funds receive by the 10th, but all qualify this with *"provided the funds remain on deposit until the end of the quarter"* (or semi-annual period). Coast Federal had converted to semi-annual *payment* or interest, but since interest is *compounded daily,* the yield is the same as if interest were paid quarterly, and no interest is lost on withdrawals because earnings are paid to date of withdrawal with *no minimum qualifying period necessary.*

Inquiry to Coast Federal in June 1968 brought confirmation that interest is paid to date of withdrawal, and that deposits earn from the first if received by the 10th of any month.

Therefore, if Coast Federal means what they say, and we feel certain that they do, the short-term investor can keep one or more small accounts open with minimum amounts, and make the major deposits on the 10th of any month, while deposits in other S & Ls, as just previously described, can only be made on the 10th of March, June, September and December.

It should also be noted that the game of "seek the highest interest" can be carried to a reductio ad absurdum. It seems to us that in accordance with Coast Federal's present offering, an annual rate of 50% is possible — on really short term deposits! Remember that interest is paid from the first on funds received by the 10th. Also recall that "earnings are paid to date of withdrawal with no minimum qualifying period necessary!" So - - - if one were to deposit $100,000 on the 10th of any month, and withdraw it on the 11th, for the one day he should earn ten days interest, or $136.98, an annual rate of exactly 50%.

The odds are probably good that Coast Federal will change their interest paying policy to conform with those of the other S & Ls. If they do, we hope that the account holders will be individually notified.

(More recently, Coast Federal, now expanded to Coast and Southern Federal Savings and Loan Association, reinstituted payment of interest quarterly rather than semi-annually.)

The last few pages have outlined how grace and bonus days, in combination with interest payable to date of withdrawal, can be exploited to the advantage of the depositor. It should be noted that even such elementary procedures as given in examples 1, 2 and 3 result in higher earnings on savings with federal insurance safety than can be attained by receiving a split fee from a money broker which could jeopardize the insurance on your savings.

CHAPTER 13

Making Money on Uncollected Funds

The judicious use of uncollected funds can inure to the advantage of the thrifty — an advantage that can be added to the benefits gained from the exploitation of grace days and daily interest.

Uncollected funds are deposits which have been made by check, draft or other instrument, and have been accepted and credited subject to collection. Most, if not all banks and savings and loan associations accept deposits by such collectable instruments, credit the account and pay interest from the date the instrument is received rather than the date the funds are collected, and allow grace days just as if cash were deposited. Thus, a check drawn against one's checking account is accepted as a deposit on October 10th; the deposit will earn interest from October 1st, but may not clear from your checking account until October 17th, and may not be received by the bank in which the deposit was made until October 20th. If both banks are in close proximity, clearance can be accomplished in a few days; if they are a great distance apart, as much as two to three weeks may have elapsed before the transaction is completed.

Particularly since withdrawals usually cannot be made against uncollected funds, and also because collection time can benefit the depositor, a few lines need be devoted to the subject.

Each bank and S&L seems to have its own policy on withdrawals against deposits that have been made with other than cash. It is strongly recommended that depositors learn the policy of each of the banks they deal with to avoid any future embarrassment or difficulty.

Some banks have a blanket rule that no withdrawal can be made against uncollected funds, even if actually collected, until thirty days after date of deposit. Some savings banks may still have this harsh rule. Others give varying preference to different types of checks, a preference that may be of importance to the depositor.

For clarity, we will call checks drawn to the order of the bank or S&L into which a deposit is to be made "First Party Checks." Checks drawn to the order of the depositor then endorsed by the depositor for deposit in the bank or S&L, will be called "Second Party Checks." Checks drawn to the order of some other person, endorsed by that person, and then endorsed by the depositor for deposit in the bank or S&L, will be called "Third Party Checks." (See Figure 19, page 135.)

Official checks usually include the following: Official and Tellers checks issued by commercial banks; Checks issued by savings banks and savings and loan associations which may be drawn against accounts in commercial banks or Home Loan Banks; Certified checks and money orders issued by banks, the Post Office and American Express.

Most checks drawn on foreign banks take a minimum of a month to clear — often far longer. Many banks will accept any *domestic Official First or Second Party check* as cash, requiring no collection time. Some require four to ten days clearance time for *local* Official *Third* Party Checks and all non-official checks. Some require ten to twenty days for *distant* Official Third Party Checks and all non-official checks. Some banks, with the initialled approval of an officer, will accept checks drawn by large corporations the same as they do Official Checks.

For those who may require withdrawals shortly after making

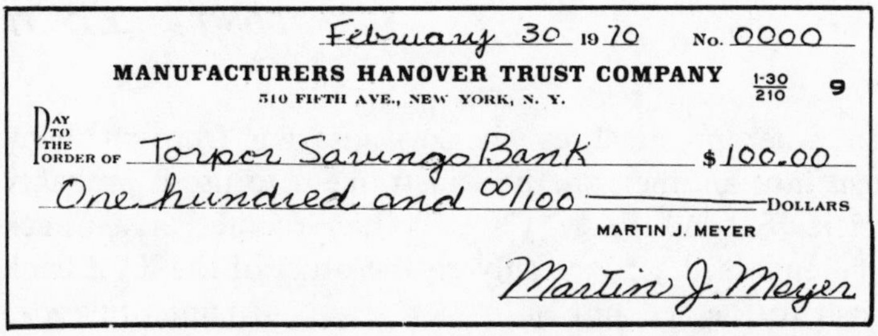

February 30 1970 No. 0000
MANUFACTURERS HANOVER TRUST COMPANY 1-30/210 9
510 FIFTH AVE., NEW YORK, N. Y.
PAY TO THE ORDER OF Torpor Savings Bank $100.00
One hundred and 00/100 DOLLARS
MARTIN J. MEYER
Martin J. Meyer

First party check

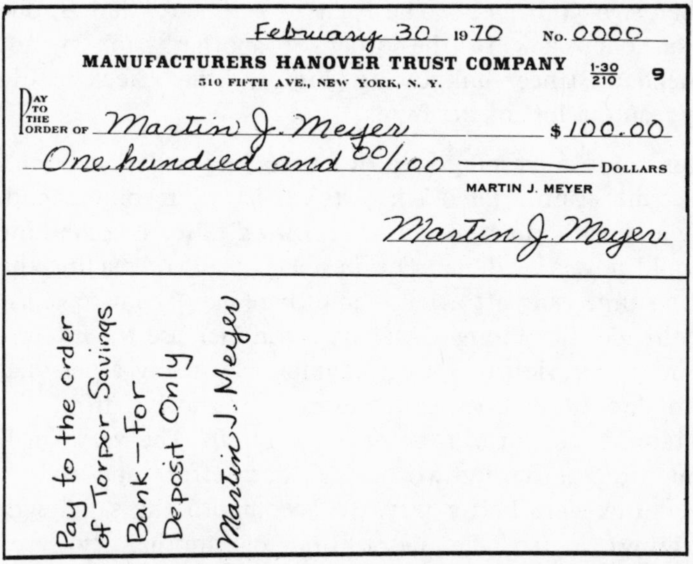

February 30 1970 No. 0000
MANUFACTURERS HANOVER TRUST COMPANY 1-30/210 9
510 FIFTH AVE., NEW YORK, N. Y.
PAY TO THE ORDER OF Martin J. Meyer $100.00
One hundred and 00/100 DOLLARS
MARTIN J. MEYER
Martin J. Meyer

Pay to the order of Torpor Savings Bank – For Deposit Only
Martin J. Meyer

Second party check

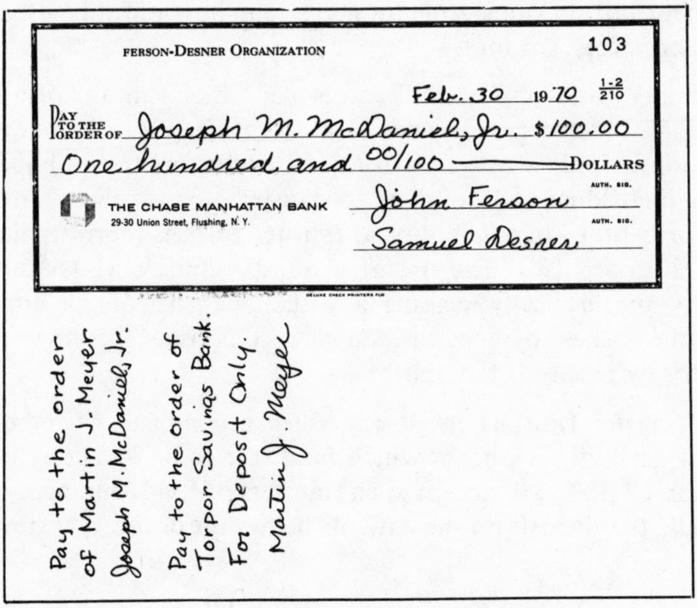

FERSON-DESNER ORGANIZATION 103
Feb. 30 1970 1-2/210
PAY TO THE ORDER OF Joseph M. McDaniel, Jr. $100.00
One hundred and 00/100 DOLLARS
THE CHASE MANHATTAN BANK
29-30 Union Street, Flushing, N. Y.
AUTH. SIG. John Ferson
AUTH. SIG. Samuel Desner
DELUXE CHECK PRINTERS FLM

Pay to the order of Martin J. Meyer
Joseph M. McDaniel, Jr.
Pay to the order of Torpor Savings Bank. For Deposit Only.
Martin J. Meyer

Third party check

Figure 19. First, Second and Third Party Checks.

a deposit, when practical, as when withdrawing from one bank to deposit into another, the best instrument to use is probably the Official Second Party Check. The Second Party Check should be endorsed as: Pay only to the order of the XYZ bank for deposit to the account of . . . . (name of depositor). Then sign your name. The First Party Check, that is, one drawn on one bank to the order of another bank is not recommended, since unknowing loss of the check could possibly result in loss of the funds.

At this point, a warning is in order. Writing a check on one's own account against *uncollected* funds is not recommended. Drawing a check against as yet *undeposited* funds is something that should *never* be done. The best laid plans of making the deposit on time gang aft agley — and there may be laws against it. If the reader has thought that he could increase the interest earned in the previously shown examples by using a personal check to deposit in one bank before withdrawing from the other in order to cover the check, *forget it!* The very small additional gain is hardly worth the time, effort and *risk* — moreover, there are better ways to accomplish the same end. Which brings us to the description of another type of instrument not previously mentioned — and how it can be used to the depositors' advantage.

Most any bank or S&L will accept deposits by means of an "Order for Transfer of Funds" or "Transfer Draft." Many institutions supply these draft forms to depositors in the hope that the individual will use them to transfer funds to their bank from some other bank. A typical transfer form is reprinted in Figure 20, page 137. The use of a transfer draft obviates the necessity of physically making a withdrawal. The bank into which one wishes to deposit the funds accomplishes this for the depositor by means of the draft.

The Transfer Draft is valid only when accompanied by the passbook or certificate from which funds are to be transferred. Any bank or S&L will accept such transfers of funds and many will credit the deposit on the date of the receipt of the Transfer

TRANSFER DRAFT

Please Transfer my account

Date _____

FROM: _____
Print Above The Name of Bank or Savings and Loan Where Account Is Now Located

ADDRESS: _____
Address of Bank or Savings and Loan Association

AMOUNT OF ☐ Balance of account (plus interest) or

$ _____ ☐ $ _____
(If not entire balance of account, fill in exact amount to be transferred)

PAY TO THE ORDER OF: _____

ENCLOSE YOUR OLD PASSBOOK
OR CERTIFICATE WITH THIS
TRANSFER DRAFT.

(Name of Bank or S & L into which account is to be transferred)

PRINT NAME _____

PRINT ADDRESS _____

Passbook No. _____

CITY & STATE _____

SIGNATURE _____

Figure 20. Typical Transfer Draft

Draft. However, some will not credit the deposit until the actual collection is made, and none will permit withdrawals until the funds are actually collected.

All of the California and Nevada S&Ls we know of, as well as some in New York and elsewhere, credit deposits and pay interest (as if the deposits were by cash or check) from date of receipt of the Transfer Draft. Thus, if the Draft arrives at the bank on October 10th, interest is earned from October 1st, even though the funds may not be collected by the bank for quite some time. This is where the depositor can pick up sizeable additional interest.

For several years quarterly transfers were made from a few daily interest (DD-DW/QQ) accounts in New York to Savings & Loan Associations in California, with each transfer mailed to arrive at the S&L in California on or just before the tenth of the months of January, April, July and October. Possibly because of the great volume of deposits handled at the beginning of each quarter which causes a log jam in processing, or possibly because such clearance time is normal, to our recollection, no funds ever cleared *out of the New York bank* before the twentieth of the month, and sometimes not until the twenty seventh or eighth.

Remembering that 5% compounded quarterly is equivalent to 5.09% simple interest, let us review what was learned from examples 1 - 3 (see pages 120 to 123). Examples 2 and 3 demonstrated that a yield of about 5.85% could be achieved by exploiting grace and bonus days together with daily interest. We are now ready to add the advantages of the use of transfer drafts.

Example 4 *

Step 1   On Oct. 1, deposit $10,000 into a New York S & L account (Acct. No. 1) paying 5% DD-DW/QQ. (E.g.:

---

* See pages 119-120 for table of symbols used to denote interest terms. DD-DW/QQ = interest from day of deposit to day of withdrawal, compounded and paid quarterly.

West Side Federal S & L, New York & Suburban Federal S & L)

Step 2 On Oct. 8, (in time to arrive by Oct. 10), mail the Acct. No. 1 passbook together with signed transfer draft for $10,000 *only,* in a previously supplied prepaid airmail envelope for deposit into an existing California S & L account (Acct. No. 2) paying 5% DD-DW/QQ (or DQ or D Semi-Annual). (E.g.: Fidelity Federal S & L, Coast Federal S & L)

Note that the minimum balance of $1 to $5 is left in Acct. No. 1, so that the account is not closed out with consequent loss of interest. Experience with a number of accounts over a period of years indicates that drafts, as sent in Step 2, did not clear out of Acct No. 1 until about the twentieth of the month. Assuming this delay, even though the actual clearance date may be a few days earlier or later, for the quarter ending in December, Acct. No. 1 earns 19 days interest on $10,000 (Oct. 1st to Oct. 20th) or $26.03, and Acct. No. 2 earns a full quarter's interest (from Oct. 1st) or $125 (actually $125.75 because of daily compounding in California) for a total of $151, a yield of 6%.

Step 3 On Jan. 10th, bring (or mail on Jan. 8th) Acct. No. 2 together with signed transfer draft for $10,000 to the New York S & L for deposit into Acct. No. 1.

Still assuming a clearance date of the twentieth of the month, by the end of March, Acct. No. 2 earns 19 days interest on $10,000 (Jan. 1st to Jan. 20th) or $26.03, while Acct. No. 1 earns the full quarter's interest on $10,000, or $125. If this procedure is continued each quarter on the 10th of April, July and October, $10,000 earns 6% per year. If the quarterly (or semi-annual) dividends are not withdrawn, but rather added to the $10,000 that is transferred each quarter, the net yield per year is 6.1%. And once the $10,000 was first deposited, only four transactions per year are necessary, all of which can be done by postage-free mail. If it is worth the trouble of filling out and mailing four transfer drafts a year, one can increase the earnings on their savings to an effective yield as high as 6.1%

merely by taking advantage of daily interest, grace days and transfer drafts.

And again, for the record, transfers of funds have been accepted by innumerable banks and savings and loan associations as of date of receipt for many years, without federal regulatory agencies prohibiting or inhibiting the practice.

The following example will only be useful if Coast Federal maintains unchanged the interest-paying policies in effect at the time of this writing and as just previously described.

Example 5

Step 1   On Oct. 1, deposit $10,000 into a New York S & L account (Acct. No. 1) paying 5% DD-DW/QQ.

Step 2   On Oct. 8, mail Acct. No. 1 passbook with transfer draft for $10,000 to Coast Federal S & L for deposit into your existing Acct. No. 2.

Step 3   On Nov. 10 *or* Dec. 10, by means of passbook and transfer draft, deposit the $10,000 into Acct. No. 1.

Because transfer drafts are probably handled more expeditiously between quarters, for Step 3 we'll assume a clearance date of the fifteenth of the month. From Step 1, Acct. No. 1 should earn 19 days interest, or $26.03. Assuming that Step 3 was performed on Dec. 10, from Step 2 Acct. No. 2 will earn interest from Oct. 1 through Dec. 15, or two months and fourteen days, for a total of $102.52, while from Step 3 Acct. No. 1 should earn interest for the full month of December, or $41.67. Adding these earnings together gives a total of over $170, or a yield at the annual rate of 6.8%. And if all available interest is added to the accounts and left for a year, continuing the procedure in succeeding quarters yields 6.9%.

At this point it may be well to offer a word of warning. Banks can and occasionally do change their interest paying and other policies without notifying depositors individually. A few years ago, one of the authors learned that First National City and Chemical Bank New York Trust had stopped paying daily interest (to date of withdrawal) at the end of the quarter when daily interest was expected but not collected. No special notice was personally received, although no doubt some form of notice was at least posted in the banks. Newly offered advantages are well publicized, retracted ones hardly at all. A recent change at one S&L, costly to numerous depositors, is a good example of how depositors can be adversely affected by this "accentuate the positive, gloss-over the negative" axiom.

In January 1967 two accounts were opened for $15,000 each (and two others for lesser amounts) at Investors Savings & Loan Association of Pasadena, California, through their broker or representative in New York. According to their representative, and in fact, Investors S&L was then paying "Interest from date of deposit if held to the end of quarter" and "Interest paid to date of withdrawal after six months." Interest was mailed quarterly, and fourth quarter '67 checks each in the sum of $188.66 and dated 12/27/67 were received, as were checks for the previous quarters. At no time was a notice received about a change in interest-paying practices, although they did send promotional material and prepaid envelopes with the interest checks. It should be noted and remembered that these accounts were opened because of the S&L's offer of interest to date of withdrawal after six months. Many other California S&L's offered the same interest to date of withdrawal, as they still do today — except that most have liberalized their terms to interest to date of withdrawal after three months instead of six, and some to true daily interest. It is also important to note that Investors S&L did not require that the account be kept open till the end of the quarter to earn interest to date of withdrawal.

On January 8, 1968, $15,000 was withdrawn from one of the accounts, the two smaller ones were also closed out, and on January 12th, $14,900 was withdrawn from the second $15,000 account. No interest was paid to date of withdrawal, but since many institutions wait till the quarter's end to pay, it was decided to wait until the end of March. The only interest received turned out to be $1.26, representing interest for the quarter on $100 in the last mentioned account.

Inquiry about the non-payment of the interest to date of withdrawal, which amounts to approximately $16 on one account and $24 on the second, brought the following reply from Investors Savings & Loan Association, Pasadena, California:

Dear Mr.

In answer to your correspondence in regards to interest payment on your savings account:

The policy of Investors Savings, effective October 1, 1967, is to pay interest on funds when held to quarter's end. These funds are compounded daily at our current annual rate of 5% which effectively yields 5.13% when held one year.

This policy has been extensively advertised in all advertising media.

In implementing this policy, we have complied with all the rules and regulations set forth by the Federal Home Loan Bank and Department of Investment, State of California.

In addition to the above, you should have received a copy of our current policy with your Statement of Earnings.

Sincerely, . . .

So while other savings & loans in southern California were liberalizing their interest policies, one revoked. It may be a good idea to check each quarter with each bank or S&L one deals with to insure against being caught short by an unpublicized and detrimental change.

Certainly this is a matter which warrants attention from both federal and state authorities to see whether existing regulations adequately protect the depositor from a bank's sudden shift of policy.

In light of the recent (Jan. 1970) moves by the Federal Reserve and Federal Home Loan Bank Boards to permit slightly higher interest rates on certificates of deposit and savings certificates, it is well to compare such savings instruments with regular passbook savings accounts.

The regular savings accounts are limited to nominal interest rates of 4½% by commercial banks and 5% by savings institutions. The advantages of these accounta are the array of grace and bonus days offered, and, most important, (barring bank insolvency) the instant availability of your funds — and with daily interest accounts, interest is earned to date of withdrawal, whenever you choose to reclaim your funds. In addition, if interest rates rise, the higher rate is automatically paid; if they fall, the lower rate prevails.

As of January 1970, certificates of deposit for one year may carry a rate of 5½%, for 2 years, 5¾%; while savings certificates issued by S & Ls and savings banks may pay ¼% above the commercial banks' rates. However, there are no grace or bonus days, and, most important, funds may not be withdrawn until the maturity date. In return for the higher rate, liquidity is lost. And the interest rate is also frozen for the term of the certificate, whether interest rates rise or fall.

Therefore, for funds that may be needed on short notice, regular savings accounts are more desirable than fixed-term deposit certificates. But for funds that can be tied up for three months or longer, the regular savings accounts offer a too-meager return, unless the interest-increasing methods described in this book are utilized.

The additional ½% Or ¾% offered through certificates which require the freezing of funds for one or two years should hardly interest the sophisticated depositor. For periods of three months or more, he can obtain, at this time, far better yields by purchasing U. S. Government obligations.

It is most interesting to note the yields offered by U.S. Bonds and Treasury Bills on January 21, 1970, the date that most commercial banks raised the yields on deposit certificates. Treasury Bills due April 22, 1970 (3 months) yielded 8% and those due July 23rd (6 months) offered 8.07% while Bonds due February 1971 yielded 7.83% — all far better yields than offered by any banks or S & Ls. Remember that U.S. Bonds and Treasury Bills are guaranteed by the full faith and credit of the U.S. Government, not just insured by a federal agency insurance corporation with questionable liquidity and possible vulnerability.

As more and more people by-pass financial intermediaries (banks) in order to earn a more equitable return on their savings, the regulatory agencies of the banking industry will, it is hoped, be forced to permit higher interest rates than they now allow.

CHAPTER 14

Your Credit Card Can Earn Money -- For You

At this point, the few steps already discussed, which help to increase the interest rate, should be summarized.

1. Quarterly or daily compounding adds to the nominal rate of 5% about 0.1% to a total of 5.1%.
2. Judicious exploitation of grace and bonus days together with daily interest to date of withdrawal can result in an additional 0.75% to a new total of 5.85%
3. In combination with the above, if Transfer Drafts are used in lieu of withdrawals and deposits, an additional average of 0.35% can be earned, now bringing the grand total to 6.1%. Just these few steps increase one's interest income by 22% as compared to 5% simple interest — because the increase from 5 to 6.1 is a 22% increase. Through one S&L, interest can be brought up to 6.9%, an increase of 38% over the 5% rate.
4. Under special circumstances and at certain times, it is possible to gain interest for short periods at rates as high as 9½% to 14%.

But 9½% over a few days is one thing, over long periods, another. On the other hand, eight percent per annum, and more, not for just a few days has been earned — and will be described in complete detail. First let's examine other features that offer increased income to the thrifty.

145

Now it's time to consider how to accomplish the seemingly impossible: a way to earn interest on funds one no longer has, on money that has already been spent. And the bank will love you for it! Because for whatever you may make, they make much more. And at no cost to either of you. Or so it seems.

This small section applies primarily to those of us who buy anything from Art Supplies to Zircons and pay for it in cash or by check. And although the bank credit card may be available only in limited areas, one may find the use of other credit cards − Diners' Club, American Express, oil company and airline credit cards − to be valuable assets (with some important exceptions). The coverage of the entire U.S. by bank credit cards is imminent because of its tremendous income potential to banks.

First National City's Charge Service states the following in their promotional brochure describing "The Everything Card."

> " 'The Everything Card' is yours without charge. You needn't bank at First National City to have this wonderful new charge service.
>
> "It needn't cost a cent to use The Everything Card. There's no application fee, no membership fee for The Everything Card. And no service charge for purchases of merchandise and services if you pay in full within 25 days of your billing date − or you can extend your payments by paying as little as 1/24th (minimum, $10) of your outstanding balance for a small service charge.
>
> "More than 30,000 merchants say, 'Use The Everything Card.' Everything from Art Supplies to Zircons is chargeable on The Everything Card, acceptable all over metropolitan New York, Westchester and Nassau Counties.
>
> "In an emergency, use The Everything Card. T.V. on the blink? Flat tire? The Everything Card can bail you out Sundays, holidays, any day of the week. Foolish not to have it.
>
> "Need a cash advance? Use The Everything Card. Present The Everything Card at any domestic branch of First National City Bank and get up to $150 cash for a

small interest payment and a transaction charge. Repay advances as fast as you like or extend payments by repaying 1/24th (minimum, $10) of the amount borrowed. That's right — you can charge a loan.

"More than 1,500,000 people will have The Everything Card. Not just First National City Bank customers, but everybody who knows the value of convenience. For payphones, carfare and such, use cash. For most other things, The Everything Card.

"One bill for everything. You get one monthly bill for everything. Pay the minimum payment shown on your statement, or pay more if you prefer. This plan is flexible. Remember, no service charge for purchases if you pay in full within 25 days of your billing date."

For this example, let's take the hypothetical case of a family with a sufficient weekly or monthly income so that an average of $100 per week, or $5,000 per year, can be used for purchases which are chargeable to the Everything Card (recently made part of the Master Charge Plan) or similar charge plan. Assume that the $100 a week previously used for cash purchases, has been kept as cash — or else put into a checking account. In either case, no interest has been earned.

But now, with the credit card, $100 per week of their total expenses will be charged instead of being paid for in cash or by check. So, on Friday October 4th, $100 can be deposited in a daily interest account, either at First National City at 4½% for convenience, or at a S&L that may offer 5% with daily interest. As of July 1st, 1968, the deposit could also be made in a Savings Bank 4¾% daily interest account. By Friday, the 11th, this $100 will have been spent, but now by credit card charge rather than by out-of-pocket cash. The balance in the bank account is still $100, and $100 is owed on the charge. But the balance earns interest, while the charge costs the family nothing!

Again, on the following Friday, October 11th, $100 of the weekly paycheck is deposited in the same account, bringing the new balance to $200. And, by the 18th, they owe $200. Each week another $100 is deposited, and each week the family owes an additional $100.

Remember, "you get one monthly bill for everything . . . no service charge for purchases if you pay in full within 25 days of your *billing* date." Let's assume a billing date of the first of each month. By the 25th of November, the daily interest savings account will have grown to $800, and the billed charges to a maximum of $400. On November 25th, and each 25th thereafter, the charges on the credit card statement, which will average about $400, should be paid from funds in the daily interest account. In that way, neither interest charges nor service charges are incurred. The $400 each month has been "borrowed" interest free until the 25th of the following month.

Is it worth the bother? Most people would agree that credit cards which offer one statement and one payment each month are far more convenient than paying for each purchase by cash or check. And most of us visit some bank once a week to cash or deposit the paycheck, so it is hardly an additional bother to deposit $100 per week more.

And one asks, as all are prone to do these days, "what's in it for me?" The first quarter you do this, you'll earn almost $6.00, and $28.00 per year thereafter. Not a great deal, but it's free, and will still pay for a good pair of shoes or a night on the town for you and your wife. Or even for a few copies of this book. And if your charges exceed $100 per week, proportionally more will be earned as daily interest.

This explanation of the use of a bank credit card was included not just to show the way to earn a few dollars. It demonstrates that banks are anxious to lend money without any charge whatsoever, provided circumstances are such that by so doing, the banks too earn money. For many years now, the credit card companies have demonstrated that, under certain circumstances, personal credit need not be usurious to be profitable. In fact, it has been proven profitable when credit is given free of interest.

It appears that we really get something for nothing, but what is it that's said about appearances? Why should any organization be anxious to extend credit and risk, without charging the beneficiary?

Just as business yields to labor and then passes the charge along to the public, so credit card plans give free credit (for a limited time) to cardholders because a third party, the merchant, pays the bill, and then some.

Credit card plans charge the merchant about 6% of the total sale — and generally don't pay the storekeeper until well after the card companies have received payment from the cardholder. Many merchants have complained that the card companies do not pay them until 90 to 120 days after the sale of merchandise. Bank charge plans pay the vendors much sooner, even immediately. So, as long as the cardholder pays the bank plan by the 25th of the month following the statement, the bank plan earns a commission or service charge totalling about 6%. But if the cardholder doesn't pay in full by the 25th, the bank collects from the cardholder 1½% per month on the unpaid balance that doesn't exceed $500, and 1% per month on the portion that exceeds $500. These are equivalent to simple annual interest rates of approximately 18% and 12% respectively!

For the bank plan, the economics are simple and impressive. If the bank lays out no money, after the 25th of the month, it makes 6% for the month. And that is not per year. It represents an interest rate of about 70% a year. Actually it is a commission or service charge. And if the bank does lend out money, by paying the merchant even though the cardholder has not paid by the 25th, it collects the 6% *plus* over 18% per annum on sums up to $500, and over 12% on the part that exceeds $500.

If all cardholders paid their bills by the 25th of the following month, the bank plan would make 6 percent per month . . . better than 70 percent per year.

If all cardholders utilized the 1½% per month credit terms, the bank plan would earn only the 6% plus 18% per year, for a total of more than 25% for a year. In practice, the yield should fall between 25% and 70%, making it readily understandable why the cards are issued free, and credit is extended until 25 days after billing date without any charge.

The major credit card companies have not charged interest if a bill is paid late. All that they do at most is limit or cut off credit. Not having to pay 1½% per month interest, many cardholders have not been compulsive about making prompt payment, so the card company waited longer. But, here again, they do not lay out the money. The merchant waits and waits for payment. But even so, the credit card companies have found it necessary to charge an annual fee for the use of their cards.

Now, back to the family that spent $100 per month via a bank credit card plan, and paid the bills on the 25th of the month following each statement. If they spent $10 a year for one of the major credit cards and were able to delay paying the monthly bill until two weeks after the 25th, they would break out about even as compared to a bank charge card, because the balance in their daily interest account would have been increased by $200, which yields $10 in interest for a year. If they could get away with not paying until a month later, an additional $10 (over the bank charge card) would be netted in a year, since their bank account balance would have been kept at $400 more than when the bank credit card was used.

To sum up: Through the use of bank credit cards, daily interest can be earned for an average of 40 days after the purchases are made. This is interest on money already spent, and the yield is infinite, since it is earnings on nonexistent funds.

* * * * *

The end of 1968 saw the absorption of First National City's Everything Card into the Master Charge plan, the Interbank Card, "the largest bank credit system in the nation with more than 1,000 member banks from coast to coast, more than 400,000 establishments at which goods and services can be charged, and over 13 million cardholders." And while the Master Charge plan is described as the largest bank credit system, its prime competitor, Bank Americard says this about itself: "America's number one credit card. Over 18,000,000 people use it. Over 400,000 places honor it . . ." (See Figure 21, below.) By September of 1969, Bank Americard could claim 550,000 places accepting their card.

America's number one credit card.

BankAmericard. Over 18,000,000 people use it. Over 400,000 places honor it. Places like restaurants, airlines, gift shops, department stores, and boutiques. Professional people honor it, too. It's the all-purpose traveling credit card.

And it's like having your own accountant. Because all your purchases are billed on one statement at the end of the month. You can pay for all purchases with just one check. Or, if you prefer, you can budget your payments over several months. And with BankAmericard, you can obtain a cash advance of up to $150.00 (depending upon your credit limit) at over 1,900 banks. The cost for BankAmericard? It's free. No membership fees. No dues. And no service charge if you pay within 25 days.

Figure 21. Bank Americard advertising

This year saw Manufacturers-Hanover Bank and Trust Co., Franklin National Bank, Marine Midland Grace Trust Company and Chemical Bank jump aboard the Master Charge plan bandwagon, while Bankers Trust Company and National Bank of North America now offer the Bank Americard, and Chase Manhattan Bank has started a device to license its Uni-Card credit card to other banks on a national basis. 1970 will witness almost every U.S. bank offering some buy-now—pay-later credit card.

The inherent risks attached to the carrying of any credit card have been well publicised. Credit card insurance has been available for modest sums, and now, Chemical Bank in New York offers this insurance free, as part of their Master Charge plan.

The year 1969 witnessed the coming of age of the bank-issued credit card, with the top three of the commercial banking industry falling heir to the potentially greatest bonanza in American financial history. It will be a tribute to ingenuity if the credit card companies can withstand the competition of the bank-backed, bank-issued credit card.

And you, the consumer, pay in full for this bonanza — to the tune of an additional price increase of about 7% — 7% added on top of continuously inflating prices.

Why?

Consider an item that the merchant must sell for $1.00 to cover costs and profit. To receive this $1.00 on a credit card sale, he must charge $1.07, the 7 cents being the approximate credit card service charge.

As greater numbers of customers use credit cards, prices are forced upward by 7%. As people pay 7% more for goods and services, they too must look to increase their spendable funds by 7%. To accomplish this end, both labor and the business man seek to increase their return through higher wages and prices. And the merchants trapped by the credit cards, being con-sumers themselves, must now raise their prices again — over and above the 7% increase — to increase their own personal spendable funds.

The credit card, in all its forms, creates a strong inflationary pressure.

The consumer can attempt to combat this pressure by refusing to use credit cards, buying only for cash, and *insisting* or receiving a 5% or 6% discount for cash at any establishment that honors credit cards. Remember, the merchant must pay the credit card issuer charges of 6% or more. As a cash customer, you are entitled to this discount since cash less 6% nets to the merchant the same as does a full price credit card sale.

What masquerades as interest-free credit is really credit at 70% per year — 6% per month. We commend consideration of this abuse in lending to Representative Patman, to the architects of the Truth in Lending Law and to any other legislator concerned with the welfare of the consumer.

The blanketing of the country with bank-issued credit cards points up a system whereby the cost of consumer credit is borne by the entire consuming population rather than by those who make use of the credit. Let the borrower pay for credit, not the merchant who thereby forces the cash customer, the general public to foot the bill. Price-fixed goods or services such as airline tickets are most unconscionable examples of the public being forced to underwrite credit costs. The vendor, such as the airline, is not permitted by law or regulation to extend a cash discount.

CHAPTER 15

How To Defer Income Taxes On Interest

Two plans which offer tax-sheltered advantages, including the deferring of income taxes on earned interest, have recently been offered by banks. The first, known as the Keogh Plan, falls within the framework of the Self-Employed Individuals Tax Retirement Act and is available for use only by those who are self-employed — doctors, lawyers, other professionals and entrepreneurs — provided that they are not employees receiving salary or wages. Partners owning more than 10% of unincorporated businesses are also eligible. Those who are eligible may set aside up to 10% of their self-employment income, to a maximum of $2,500, for placement into an approved retirement fund. Under certain circumstances, additional voluntary contributions up to a like sum may be made.

Retirement plans, in their various forms are beyond the scope of this work. Those interested in setting up such plans would be well advised to study any of several books on the subject (e.g.: Tax Saving Plans for Self-Employed, ©1966, Commerce Clearing House, Inc., Chicago, Ill. 60646), or to discuss the matter with their attorney or accountant.

However, a few lines will be devoted to the basic concept behind the Keogh Plan. Excluding additional voluntary contributions, the individual's contribution to his retirement plan, up to $2,500 per year, is tax-exempt in the year the amount is paid into the fund. This sum can be deducted from income before computing income taxes for the year. All of the interest and/or dividends earned by the fund are likewise not taxed in the year they are earned. This permits the funds to grow at a more rapid rate, since there is no annual deduction from the principal or interest for payment of taxes.

In addition, although extra voluntary contributions to a fund are not deductible, once this after-tax money is in the fund, the earnings thereon are not taxed in the year earned.

Thus, you save in two ways through the use of a Keogh Plan.

1. The taxes you save by tax deduction of your contribution to the plan, and
2. The taxes you save by having the funds build up over the years tax free.

Once your plan has started, you cannot withdraw funds from the plan until the minimum retirement age of 59½ (or prior total disability) without paying penalties. However, you have the option of not making contributions in any years, without penality.

Upon retirement – after age 59½ or upon total disability – income taxes must be paid on all sums in the fund that have accrued with tax exemption. This amounts to the sum of all regular contributions plus all dividends and interest earned in the fund. Since income taxes were paid on the voluntary contributions, this sum is not subject to income taxes a second time.

If retirement benefits are taken in the form of annuity payments, the general rules, applicable to all annuities, determines the tax to be paid.

If the retirement fund is taken as a lump sum, special tax benefits are provided. The entire sum, less the total amount of voluntary contributions made with after-tax monies, are fully taxable in the year received – but are subject to a special averaging provision. The taxable lump sum is taxed at a rate of five times the additional income tax due on 20% of the total lump sum, when this 20% portion is added to other taxable income.

As an example, if, upon retirement under the Keogh plan, the fund amounts to a total of $150,000, representing $34,000 in voluntary contributions which were not subject to tax deduction, $50,000 in tax-deducted regular contributions and $66,000 in untaxed interest earned in the fund, only the latter two items, or a total of $116,000, is taxable. Assume that the individual, in retirement, has a taxable income of $5,000 in the year, on which he would owe an income tax of $810 (not considering sur-taxes, state or city taxes). The taxpayer then adds to his taxable income 20% of the taxable portion of his retirement fund, or 1/5 of $116,000, or $23,200.

On the first	$ 3,000,	the tax rate is 19% or	$ 570
On the next	4,000,	the tax rate is 22% or	880
On the next	4,000,	the tax rate is 25% or	1,000
On the next	4,000,	the tax rate is 28% or	1,120
On the next	4,000,	the tax rate is 32% or	1,280
On the next	4.000,	the tax rate is 36% or	1,440
On the next	200,	the tax rate is 39% or	76
Total	$23,200		$6,366

The total sum of $6,366 is multiplied by 5, for a total additional tax of $32,130 (in addition to the $810 tax on regular income.)

Therefore, of the total fund of $150,000, $32,130 is deducted for taxes, leaving $117,870 to the retired person.

The Keogh plan is advantageous because in most cases tax brackets are materially lower at the time benefits are received than they were when contributions were made to the plan. The ability to have funds earn interest or dividends for many years while income taxes are deferred is a very real advantage. It permits you to earn interest on those amounts which would have been paid in taxes — and when you retire, you pay only a portion of those bonus earnings to the tax collector. The major disadvantage of the Keogh retirement plan is that once the funds are in, you can't retrieve any portion of the fund, without being subject to monetary penalties. There is one other drawback. The individual cannot be the trustee of his own fund, nor can he appoint any trustee other than a bank or an insurance company. However, the individual has the right to switch from one bank or insurance company trustee to another at any time. Even mutual funds offering the Keogh Plan use a bank (or insurance company) as trustee of the funds.

Consider this example of a married individual with taxable income of $25,000 a year who

(1) Takes $5,000 of his income each year and deposits it in a bank at 5% (simple interest), and pays the income taxes each year on the deposited principal and interest out of the banked savings.

(2) Takes $5,000 of this income each year and deposits it into a Keogh plan retirement fund as a

a. $2,500 regular contribution that is tax deductible and a

b. $2,500 less $800 for income tax = $1,700 net voluntary additional contribution to the retirement fund.

At the end of twenty years, from the banked savings [see (1) above], the owner would have $96,335, a sum that is not taxable because taxes on principal and interest were paid each year. It should be remembered that the owner could use any part of his banked savings at any time without penalty.

Upon retirement, after contributing to his Keogh plan fund for twenty years [see (2) above], the plan has a total of $147,143. Of this sum, taxes have previously been paid on $34,000 — leaving a taxable portion of $113,143, plus an untaxable portion of $34,000. If this fund is taken by the owner in a lump sum, using the same assumptions as in the previous example, a total tax of $30,725 would be due, leaving a net of $116,418. This after-tax sum is almost 20% more than

$96,335, the sum in the bank accounts that didn't enjoy the tax-deferring feature of the Keogh plan. The only disadvantage is that once the funds were put into the Keogh plan fund, the owner could not make use of any part of the funds therein without incurring serious penalties.

An additional disadvantage to the Keogh plan recently became evident. On February 10th, 1970, shortly after higher rates on deposit and savings certificates were permitted, a holder of a Keogh plan fund requested his New York savings bank to move his funds from 5% accounts into 2 year, 6% certificates. The manager, an officer of the bank to whom he was talking, refused, stating that these higher rate certificates were not being issued for Keogh plan accounts. With the bank as trustee, the retirement plan owner had no recourse — except to appoint some other bank as his plan's trustee and have the funds transferred.

* * * * *

The second plan, which permits deferring of taxes on interest earned, has been tested by a few banks for a couple of years and is now widely available. These accounts are known variously as Deferred Income Bonds, Deferred Income Certificates and Deferred Income Golden Passbook Accounts, and are offered for periods of from two years to just short of fifteen years (the time required to double one's money at 5% compounded daily).

First National City Bank's version of deferred income accounts is described in Fig. 22, page 160.

Note that this type of account is recommended by the offering banks for those who expect to retire before the full term of the account, or expect to be in lower tax brackets at the time the account reaches maturity. Under such conditions, the advantage of deferring income, and therefore taxes, is self-evident. But is is interesting to examine the possibility of some advantages to those whose incomes and tax rates will be the same during each of the years through maturity of the deferred income account.

Deferred Income
Golden Passbook Account

Will your tax bracket be lower 2 to 10 years from now? Our Deferred Income Golden Passbook may help you save money in income taxes on the interest your savings earn.

What is the Deferred Income Golden Passbook?

It's First National City's popular Golden Passbook Account with a new feature that lets you defer paying income taxes on your interest until a specified maturity date, when you may be in a more favorable tax bracket.

Your money earns interest at the rate of 5% per annum, compounded and credited quarterly. Your interest income is not taxable, however, until a maturity date you select—2 to 10 years from now. And the 5% interest rate is guaranteed until that date—up to 10 full years. This means that your initial deposit will increase by almost 65% if held to the maximum maturity.

Under the provisions of this plan, the customer does not have access to his principal or interest until a specified maturity date. Therefore, it is the opinion of counsel that taxes do not have to be paid until that time.

Who benefits?

If you anticipate that your income tax bracket will be lower at some point during the next ten years, you can benefit from this new plan.

You can have more than one Deferred Income Golden Passbook Account, with different maturity dates, to spread your earnings over different years of reduced income and lower tax brackets.

Though this plan is primarily designed for those who plan to retire within the next ten years, it is equally suited for anyone, a professional athlete, for instance, who anticipates a decrease in income in a few years.

What will your income be 2-10 years from now? If you then will be in a lower tax bracket, consider the Deferred Income Golden Passbook.

The Brass Tacks of the Deferred Income Golden Passbook

1. Minimum deposit of $500. Additional deposits of at least $50 may be made at any time.

2. Select a maturity date—2 to 10 years from now. All deposits made to the account will mature on that date.

3. The maturity date may be extended once, but not to more than 10 years from the opening date of the account.

4. Interest is paid from day of deposit at the 5% annual rate and is compounded and credited four times a year.

5. The 5% interest rate is guaranteed until maturity.

6. Neither the principal nor the interest can be withdrawn prior to maturity except in the case of a bona fide emergency, at which time the interest earned on the amount withdrawn may become taxable.

7. All or any portion of the balance not withdrawn at maturity will become a regular Golden Passbook Account.

8. Deposits may be made at any branch of First National City Bank, or by mail.

9. Systematic Saver Service is available with minimum monthly transfers of $50 from your Personal Checking Account to your Deferred Income Golden Passbook Account.

Fig. 22 FNCB Deferred Income Golden Passbook Account

For this example, we assume the depositor to be in the 30% tax bracket, and we will compare after-tax earnings on $1,000 put into the bank in a regular account at 5% compounded semi-annually against after-tax earnings on a 10-year deferred income account at the same rate.

With an ordinary savings account, taxes must be paid in the year interest is earned. At a 5% interest rate, the person in a 30% tax bracket pays 30% of the interest rate to the tax collector, so the effective earning rate.is only 3½% after taxes. Therefore, after 10 years, and after payment of income taxes, the $1,000 will have grown to only $1,414.77. However, the deferred income account will have grown to $1,638.61, but taxes of 30% of $638.61 will be due. Deducting this tax of $191.58 from the total of $1,638.61 leaves a net of $1,447.03 as compared to $1,414.77 from the regular savings account.

Therefore, the deferred income account yielded 8% more interest than did the regular savings account — all because interest was earned on untaxed interest with the former account, while interest was earned on after-tax interest with the latter. With a depositor in the 30% tax bracket, regular savings at a 5% interest rate yield an effective after-tax rate of 3½%, while by use of a ten-year deferred income account, the effective yield is slightly better than 3¾%.

The great disadvantage of the deferred income account: the depositor does not have access to his principal or interest until the maturity date — a very high price to pay for the slight earning advantage.

Another possible disadvantage: Those who had been lured into buying income-tax-deferred certificates or accounts prior to the January 1970 interest rate increase are in a particularly unfortunate position. Many are stuck with maturities of up to 15 years at 5%, when these funds could now be earning 6% at the same banks — and they will not receive even the 5% interest until the maturity date. Referring to Figure 22, Page 160, (column 2, number 6) note that "neither the principal nor the interest can be withdrawn prior to maturity *except in the case of a bona fide emergency,* at which time the interest earned on the amount withdrawn may become taxable." If other banks have the same "exit" clause in their income-tax-deferred accounts, those who are tied to distant maturity dates may do well to manufacture a "bona fide emergency" and withdraw their funds.

Unfortunately, neither the bank-administered Keogh plan retirement funds nor the deferred income accounts offer you the chance to keep pace with inflation. Whether we look back over the last twenty years, the last two years or the last two months, we see that the value of the dollar has been so eroded by inflation that even were there to be no taxes whatsoever on interest earned, at 5% we lose, not gain. And, at this writing, the upward wage-price spiral shows no signs of abatement — to the contrary, it is accelerating.

CHAPTER 16

19% -- !   25% -- ?

The importance of the economic role played by the brokers in assisting the West in obtaining needed bank deposits has been discussed. The thrifty profited by increasing the yield on their savings, gaining higher interest rates in California or Nevada and obtaining additional income from the brokers. Although the cost to the Western S&Ls was high, it was less costly, proved more efficient and obtained more in dollar volume than any other alternate method. At the same time, it was pointed out, Eastern banks had an excess of "idle" funds, yet the movement of these idle funds from East to West aroused the enmity of the Eastern banking establishment.

More than a hundred thousand people profited from this opportunity for greater returns. On average, depositors dealing through brokers earned a total of 5¼% as compared to 4% that they had been earning in the East. Since the average savings of these depositors was about $6,000, their income from this source was increased from $240 to $315 per year, or $75 per year, which is not a particularly impressive sum when viewed from the individual depositor's standpoint. Of course, brokers handling the deposits of tens of thousands of depositors, made millions.

Among the many clients of the brokers, several saw an opportunity to push this average return of 5¼% up to 15%, yes even to 25%! This great a yield, coupled with the safety of federal insurance of the principal, may seem unbelievable. How this was accomplished shall be described in detail from records made available to the authors. However, some background information must first be given.

Early 1966 saw the start of our current "tight money" era. Prior to that time, loan funds were readily available at attractive interest rates from most Eastern metropolitan banks. Bankers widely sought loan applications from anyone who had a reasonable credit rating. Businessmen were deluged with these solicitations. Memory is short — it's hard to believe that this abundance of credit funds existed just a few years ago.

Of most interest to the people whose operations will be described, was the willingness of some Eastern banks to make loans collateralized by California savings and loan association passbooks, and on occasion at interest rates nominally slightly less than the interest rates paid on these S&L passbooks. When the California S&Ls were paying 4.85%, some New York banks were willing to make collateralized loans at 4.75%, while others asked 5%.

The uninitiated depositor would assume that if money can be borrowed at 4.75% and deposited at 4.85%, there alone a profit would be made. This is not so. Those who were looking to earn between 15 and 25 percent on their money were not novices. They were aware that interest is *deducted in advance* on short term money. The deduction of interest in advance increases the effective annual interest rate. Thus, a one-year loan at 5% with interest taken in advance, results in an effective rate of 5.263%.

Banks use one other method to increase their effective rate or actual yield. When banks quote an annual interest rate, they create for this purpose a 360-day year, not the actual 365-day year! By so doing, the banks increase their return by one seventy-third, so that a quoted rate of 5% is an actual rate of 5.07%.

Thus, adding the cost to the borrower of interest discounted in advance plus the cost of the five additional days, a one-year loan at 5% actually costs 5-1/3%.

Parenthetically, but interesting to note, is the fact that banks charge interest in advance when lending but pay interest at the end when borrowing, and charge interest for a 360-day year while they pay interest for a 365-day year, (366 days on leap years).

With this background information, a description of the operations planned by the would-be borrowers in search of a 15% to 25% return can be started. Two married couples, Mr. and Mrs. A and B, formed what we shall call "Group I." Among them, the individuals in Group I had ten $10,000 accounts or a total of $100,000 in California savings and loan associations which were then paying 4.85% interest, compounded or paid quarterly. For placing the accounts through a broker, they had received a fee of ½%, or $500. They, as individuals or in their capacities as business men, had been solicited by a number of banks as potential borrowers.

As the first step, Group I made arrangements for loans with a few banks, these loans to be collateralized using their S&L passbooks. (Once all arrangements were made, the actual taking of the loans was to come later.)

The rates proposed to be charged by the New York banks varied from 4¾% to 5% for collateralized loans. Group I wanted to pay the interest on the bank loans with the interest they received at the end of each quarter from their S&L passbook accounts. Not paying interest in advance would save them money. In addition, by borrowing in round sums of $50,000 or $100,000 without interest deducted therefrom, bookkeeping was much simpler for Group I. The banks agreed that the interest payments could be made at the end of each quarter instead of taking the interest in advance, as was customary. The banks insisted, however, that interest rates would be figured for a 360-day year. So far so good. Group I could obtain loans at 4¾% to 5% based on a 360-day year, or an effective rate of 4.81% to 5.07%, with interest payable at the end of each three months.

The group then discussed with the broker what fees he would pay, were Group I to deposit $50,000 to $100,000 every month through the broker. A fee of 1% was agreed upon, with the understanding that a pro-rata refund would be made to the broker were the accounts closed prior to having been on deposit for a year. The group had now created the basis for a profitable business.

However, there still remained a problem of risk. The members of Group I, as partners or individuals, would be collectively and individually responsible for the repayment of the bank loans. True, the loans were fully collateralized by S&L passbooks, but were the S&Ls industry to come upon hard days, they could eliminate payment of interest or delay repayment of principal. Were this circumstance to arise, the Eastern banks that had made loans to Group I would look to the individual partners for payment.

As partners of Group I, they were exposed to possible personal liability, but by incorporating Group I, this hazard would be avoided. Since the loans were to be fully collateralized, the banks offered no objection to making the loans to a corporation rather than to a partnership, so the business was incorporated as "Group I, Inc.," the sole function of the corporation being to take the loans from the Eastern banks. Small checking accounts in the corporate name were opened in each of the banks from which Group I, Inc. intended to borrow money.

The business of earning a minimum of 15% on banked savings was ready to start. The individual members of Group I put up or hypothecated five of their passbooks, totalling $50,000, as collateral for the first loan. Interest earned on these five accounts was to revert to the individuals who owned them, so there would be no loss of interest income to the individuals. However, the partners in Group I did lend a total of about $1,000 to the skeleton corporation, Group I, Inc., to cover incorporation costs and small balances in each of the several checking accounts opened.

With $1,000 "invested," and borrowing power of $50,000, the operation was ready to commence. Each account was to be for $10,000, and each was to be in individual, joint and partnership names so that each account enjoyed complete insurance coverage. (It should be noted that insurance regulations were changed September 1, 1967, so that after April 15, 1968, many of these accounts would no longer have been completely insured were they still in existence.) Under the then existing insurance regulations, the number of completely insured accounts Group I could maintain in any one S&L was astounding. Below is a partial list of accounts the group could maintain in any one S&L, with each account fully insured to the then existing $10,000 limit.

Individual Accounts (4)

Mr. A.   Mrs. A   Mr. B   Mrs. B

Joint Accounts (11)

Mr. A or Mrs. A   Mr. B or Mrs. B
Mr. A or Mr. B   Mrs. A or Mrs. B
Mr. A or Mrs. B   Mr. B or Mrs. A
Mr. A or Mrs. A or Mr. B   Mr. A or Mrs. A or Mrs. B
Mr. B or Mrs. B or Mr. A   Mr. B or Mrs. B or Mrs. A
Mr. A or Mrs. A or Mr. B or Mrs. B

Corporate Account (1)

Group I, Inc.

Trust Accounts (4)

Mr. A, Trustee of Trust for the benefit of Group I, Inc.
Mr. B, Trustee of Trust for the benefit of Group I, Inc.
Mrs. A, Trustee of Trust for the benefit of Group I, Inc.
Mrs. B, Trustee of Trust for the benefit of Group I, Inc.

Partnership Accounts (11)

Same as joint accounts above, except "and" was substituted for "or," and "a partnership" was added to the title of the account as "Mr. A *and* Mrs. A *and* Mr. B, a partnership."

On April 10, 1964, Group I, Inc., borrowed $50,000 from Commercial Bank No. 1, at 4¾% *interest payable after the end of each 3 months,* and had the funds deposited into Group I, Inc.'s account in the same bank. On the same day they mailed checks for $20,000 to Sterling Savings & Loan Association, Riverside, California, and $30,000 to Mutual Savings & Loan Association, Pasadena, California. It should be remembered that in those years the S&Ls advertised "deposits *postmarked* by the 10th of any month earn from the first of the month."

This first move should be thoroughly examined in order to understand the entire operation.

By taking the loan on April 10th, they paid interest only from April 10th, while by mailing the deposit checks on April 10th, they earned interest from April 1st, or ten free days. Since it was intended to keep the new S&L accounts for only one year, and to close them at the end of March, a full year's interest would be collected on the 5 S&L accounts, while only 355 days interest would be paid for the loan. Therefore, on the 5 accounts of $10,000 each, at 4.85%, $2,425 total interest would be received in four quarterly payments. And on the $50,000 borrowed in order to open the accounts, at 4¾% for 355 days, total interest of $2,342 in four quarterly payments had to be paid. The difference between interest received and interest paid represented a profit of $83. In addition, Group I received a $500 fee from the broker, or 1% of the $50,000 deposited into S&Ls the broker represented.

Summarizing, on the five original personal accounts of Mr. and Mrs. A and B, totaling $50,000, the depositors received in one year $2,425 in interest and a $250 fee from the broker's advertising agency. On the first borrow-deposit transaction, they would earn $83 profit on interest plus a $500 fee from the broker, thus:

Interest on $50,000 of personal accounts	=	$2,425
Fee from Broker	=	250
1st Group I Interest Profit	=	83
1st Group I Fee from Broker	=	500

Total　　$3,258

And this was only the beginning of the building of the pyramid.

Group I noticed that the check for $20,000 sent to Sterling S&L on April 10th didn't clear from their account until April 21st, and the $30,000 check to Mutual S&L didn't clear until April 22nd. This, of course, made Commerical Bank No. 1 happy, because they were collecting interest on the Group I loan while the funds were still in the bank, in the form of a $50,000 balance in Group I, Inc.'s checking account. Of course it also presented an opportunity to Group I for still greater earnings on future transactions.

When Group I received the five new passbooks from Sterling & Mutual S&L Associations, they assigned the passbooks to Commercial Bank No. 2, where they arranged a $50,000 loan *effective May 14th* at 5% interest. *On May 10th* they mailed checks for $20,000 and $30,000 to Safety S&L and Verdugo S&L respectively, both in Los Angeles. These accounts were planned to be kept open for a year and two months, until the end of June, 1965, since interest on them was only paid quarterly at the time.

The total interest to be received during the fourteen months on the five new accounts at 4.85% figured to be $2,829, while interest cost for the period of 14 months, less 14 days, at 5%, would be about $2,819. Interest earned, less interest cost, netted a profit of $10, and Group I received another broker's fee of $500.

Obviously, things were running well. The two commercial banks were happy with the loans. At a time when money was a glut on the Eastern market, the banks were able to make loans without risk, because every passbook was covered by FSLIC insurance. Bank No. 1 let Group I know that it would gladly take on more loan business – a lot more. The California Savings & Loans were happy with the new accounts. All this was happening less than a year after the infamous regulations had been passed, and the West was crying for money. The broker was happy. He was receiving 2% for every account, was paying Group I 1%, kept 1% for himself, and exerted no labor or expenses. And Group I was happy. Without risk, and only the work of signing a note and sending off deposits once a month, they were already earning over $500 per month.

So they doubled up. Remember that the partners had $100,000 in personal S&L accounts originally, and used only $50,000 of it as collateral for the first loan. Now they brought the remaining five personally owned passbooks for $50,000, plus the five new passbooks from Safety and Verdugo S&Ls to Commerical Bank No. 1 and arranged another loan, this time for $100,000, effective *June 15th* at 4¾%.

At this point one may wonder why the banks didn't do all this themselves, and keep for themselves the income that Group I was making. The reasons are many. Firstly, they probably weren't aware of what Group I was doing. Secondly, if they were aware, it was more practical to allow Group I to be the middle man because: One, it looked better on the books of the bank to show profitable collateralized loans than deposits in, of all places, savings and loan associations. If anything, it's the savings and loans that keep their cash in commercial banks, not vice versa. Two, if the banks had deposited directly in the S&Ls, their total insurance would have been only $10,000 in each S&L, while through the Group I method, all funds were insured. And, in addition, why should Eastern banks demonstrate confidence in Western savings and loans by depositing uninsured funds? Do business with the devil, but don't praise him. And, if possible, do it through an intermediary.

But when a similar situation arose with a bank rather than a S&L, banks jumped in head first. At one point, brokers started peddling certificates of deposit of the San Francisco National Bank. For sizeable deposits the brokers were offering as much as 2% or 2½% above the 4½% interest rate of the certificates. Group I didn't bite at the bait, but at least two of the New York banks did. One to the tune of about $300,000, the other for well over two million. This was not legitimate money-raising as practiced by the western S&L industry, this was a set up for a killing. Surveillance by the regulatory agencies should have prevented it. Perhaps everyone had been too busily involved in the harrassment of the S&Ls, perhaps some people in high places had an ax to grind, but the SFNB was left to clear sailing. People and banks lost a lot of money before the SFNB folded on January 22, 1965. It was buried as quietly as possible. Needless to say, the New York banks, bypassing an intermediary like the Group I, lost heavily. FDIC insurance eventually paid off to the maximum of $10,000 per insured account, more fully described in Part I, Chapter V. Years later, we understand that general creditors (like the two New York banks) regained 55 cents per dollar from the SFNB in liquidation.

But now back to the Group I activity, and their $100,000 4¾% loan as of June 15th. On *June 10th* they mailed checks for: $10,000 to Washington S&L, Hollywood, California; $40,000 to United S&L in Inglewood; $40,000 to Rio Hondo S&L in South Gate; and $10,000 to Mutual S&L in Pasadena. These accounts were to be kept open until the end of June, 1965, for thirteen months, that is, to the end of the quarter for interest earning purposes.

Interest to be received for the thirteen months on the ten new accounts at 4.85% figured to be $5,154, while interest cost for the thirteen months less 15 days (loan effective June 15th) was to be about $4,948, yielding an interest profit of $256. Again a broker's fee, this time $1,000, was to be paid to Group I. (1% of the $100,000 deposited into the S&Ls.)

Effective *July 16* another $100,000 was borrowed from Commercial Bank No. 3 at 5% against the collateral of the 10 newest S&L passbooks received from the June 10th deposits. For one year, interest earning figured as $4,850, interest cost from July 16 as $4,850, but again there was the broker's fee of $1,000. This $100,000 was deposited as: $30,000 to Sterling S&L in Riverside; $20,000 to Washington S&L in Hollywood; $40,000 to Surety S&L in Burbank; and $10,000 to Mutual S&L in Pasadena, all deposits having been mailed on July 10th to earn interest from July 1st.

August 17th brought still another $100,000 from Commercial Bank No. 1 at 4¾%, with total profit between net interest and broker's fee over $1,250, and the new S&L accounts distributed among Sterling in Riverside, Beneficial in Oakland, Washington in Hollywood, Enterprise in Compton, Verdugo in Sunland and United in Inglewood.

Here it can be noted that each month the borrowing date was moved back but deposits were sent on the 10th of the month to earn interest from the first. Group I had noted that their checks usually cleared out of their accounts about the 23rd of the month, so why not use this to some monetary advantage? When they arranged for a loan they specified a date for the loan to be effective with the provision that should a check come back before the proposed date of the loan, the loan would be made earlier and the funds deposited to the account so that all checks would clear, none would "bounce" for want of funds.

September 17th brought $50,000 and the 21st another $50,000 as loans, to a total of $100,000 from Bank No. 4 at 5%. Deposits were made into Lincoln S&L in L.A., and Safety, Verdugo and Enterprise as previously mentioned.

And by October, Bank No. 1 told Group I it would be happy to get all the business at 4¾%! And as a service to their corresponding banks in the east and midwest, parts of the loans would be "laid off" to them so that some of the idle funds in those banks would become profitable.

This went on month after month, with deposits of $100,000 per month yielding net earnings of over $1,250 per month exclusive of the interest earnings of the original ten accounts of Group I.

When the accounts were a year old, although held by the banks as collateral, the accounts were transferred to other savings and loan associations, thus earning new fees of $500 on the first two groups of five accounts each, and $1,000 on each of the following groups of ten accounts. And during the first year of operation, it became no longer necessary to keep accounts open for thirteen or fourteen months if they were opened between quarters, since by then many of the S&Ls were offering interest to date of withdrawal after six months. Accounts in the Western S&Ls were kept for only one year, the minimum time agreed upon with the broker.

However, by the middle of 1966, money had become sufficiently tight that bank interest rates were raised to a point where it was no longer highly profitable to continue. So, the banks closed out the S&L accounts they held as collateral, were completely repaid, and Group I was left with its original $100,000 plus all of the profits it had made since April 1964. Except for the first two months, profits averaged better than $1,200 per month, and in the second year about $2,000, since during the second year, borrowings and deposits increased to $200,000 a month.

Based on $100,000 that earned only $4,850 in interest, and adding about $14,000 per year profit from the operation, *Group I earned 19% on their money, and even more after the first year!* And, at the time, everyone was happy — the banks, the S&Ls, the broker and the partners in Group I.

Group II differed from Group I only in that a number of people each supplied one $10,000 passbook plus $100 toward organization expense and maintenance of checking accounts. Each member was free to recover his original passbook at any time and thus leave the group. They borrowed the funds almost exclusively from Commercial Bank No. 1, and, as did Group I, borrowed and deposited each month. Perusal of the records of Group II showed that their earnings were comparable to those of Group I.

Table 1 demonstrates the costs, income, and net earnings from an operation patterned after those of Group I. Not included is the interest income of $1,212.50 each quarter on the original passbooks owned by the individuals and used as collateral for the initial loans. Also exluded is the brokerage fee income earned when the original personally owned accounts were opened or transferred. Only the first six months of operation are included in the chart, but it should be realized that the procedure was repeated month after month until the end of the first year of operation. By that time, most of the California S&Ls were paying interest to date of withdrawal (after funds were on deposit for six months). At the start of the second year, the ten new passbooks received from the March 10, 1965 deposit were to be given five each to Bank No. 1 and Bank No. 2, to increase the original loans of $50,000 each to $100,000 each. After new accounts were opened with this $100,000, the ten new passbooks were to be exchanged for the ten books originally assigned to Bank No. 1 and Bank No. 2 the year before. At this point, the partners of the Group could have received their original $100,000 back, yet had S&L passbooks for $1,200,000, owed $1,200,000 to the Bank and continued to earn $1,200 per month *with no investment* any more. On the 10th of each month, as passbooks became one year old, the Banks transferred the accounts to other S&Ls, rather than closing the accounts. This move not only earned the Group the brokerage fee of $1,000 each month, but they also picked up the additional daily interest from the accounts being closed. Exactly how this additional daily interest can be gained is explained fully in Chapter 10. Briefly, each new account earned interest from the first of the month. However, the funds were not actually withdrawn from the old accounts until about the sixteenth of the month, so an additional sixteen days of interest were earned on the old accounts at the same time that interest was being earned on the new ones. That amounted to double interest for half a month, which was more than enough to pay for the slightly higher cost of 5% loans based on 360 days compared to earnings of 4.85% interest based on a full year.

Because money is now tight throughout the country, the opportunities to duplicate the results obtained by Groups I and II are currently non-existent. But the tight-money era of today is not the usual condition prevailing in the financial community. More often there are areas of excess money supply at the same time as there are areas that suffer from a dearth of available funds. When this more normal condition again prevails, the likes of Groups I and II may again be able to operate very profitably.

Meanwhile, the thrifty must use whatever other means are available to increase their return on investments to, at the very least, compensate for their loss of buying-power due to the erosion of inflation.

Table 1

Operation	Date of Transaction	Interest Cost $	Interest Income $	Fee Income $	Cumulative Income $
No. 1. Assign $50,000 of S&L passbooks to borrow $50,000 from Bank No. 1, @ 4¾%	4/10/64				
No. 2. Send $50,000 checks to open S&L accounts with interest from 4/1/64	4/10/64				
No. 3. Assign passbook from No. 2 above and borrow $50,000 from Bank No. 2 @ 5%	5/14/64			500	
No. 4. Send $50,000 checks to open S&L accounts with interest from 5/1/64	5/10/64				
No. 5. Assign $50,000 of original S&L passbooks plus $50,000 passbooks from No. 4 above and borrow $100,000 from Bank No. 1 @ 4¾%	6/15/64			500	
No. 6. Send $100,000 checks to open S&L accounts, interest from 6/1/64				1000	

Description	Date				
No. 7. Interest rec'd on S&L accounts from No. 2 above (3 mos. int.) from No. 4 above (2 mos. int.) from No. 6 above (1 mo. int.)	6/30/64		606 404 406		2357
No. 8. Interest paid on loans from: No. 1 above (81 days @4¾%) No. 3 above (47 days at 5%) No. 5 above (15 days @ 4¾%)		535 326 198			
TOTALS		1059	1416	2000	
No. 9. Assign passbooks from No. 6 above and borrow $100,000 from Bank No. 3 @ 5%	7/16/64				
No. 10. Send $100,000 checks to open S&L accounts, interest from 7/1/64	7/10/64			1000	
No. 11. Assign passbooks from No. 10 above and borrow $100,000 from Bank No. 1 @ 4¾%	8/16/64				
No. 12. Send $100,000 to open S&L accounts, interest from 8/1/64	8/10/64			1000	
No. 13. Assign passbooks from	[9/17/64]				

Operation	Date of Transaction	Interest Cost $	Interest Income $	Fee Income $	Cumulative Income $
No. 12 above and borrow $100,000 from Bank No. 4 @ 5%	[9/21/64]				
No. 14. Send $100,000 checks to open S&L accounts, interest from 9/1/64	9/10/65			1000	
No. 15. Interest rec'd on S&L accounts	9/30/64				
from No. 2 (3 mos. interest)			606		
No. 4 (3 mos. interest)			606		
No. 6 (3 mos. interest)			1223		
from No. 10 (3 mos. interest)			1221		
No. 12 (2 mos. interest)			811		
No. 14 (1 mo. interest)			404		
No. 16. Interest paid on loans from	9/30/64				
No. 1 (92 days @ 4¾%)		607			
No. 3 (92 days @ 5%)		639			
No. 5 (92 days @ 4¾%)		1214			
No. 9 (76 days @ 5%)		1056			
No. 11 (44 days @ 4¾%)		581			
No. 13 (9 and 13 days @ 5%)		153			
TOTALS		$5309	$6287	$5000	$5978

CHAPTER 17

8% Per Annum -- Now

The information included so far demonstrates that the banking industry can afford to pay rates beyond the nominal limits set by the Federal Reserve, the FDIC and the Home Loan Bank — *and that banks actually do pay them.* Were this all the information to be divulged, the average depositor would probably consider it worthwhile. But it's not all. A new, dynamic, highly profitable opportunity will now be discussed in minute detail. Depositors can earn up to 8% or 9%, and not just for a few days, with large sums. But first two widely advertised plans must be disposed of.

The first, offered primarily by the West Coast savings and loan industry, offers a ¼% bonus after funds (in excess of $1,000 to $5,000 minimum) have been on deposit for three years. A typical advertisement reads: "On new bonus accounts you get an additional ¼% per annum on accounts held 36 months. Bonus accounts must be opened in minimum amounts of $1,000 or in multiples of $1,000."

Remembering that 5% compounded daily yields 5.13% in a year, note that the ¼% bonus is not added or compounded until *after three years.* This is the exact opposite of compounding, so the effective yield on this ¼% is measurably less than ¼% compounded daily, quarterly, or even annually. It is only after three years that the ¼% is compounded.

Also remember that the bonus ¼% *may be* guaranteed, but the basic rate of 5% definitely is not! From the view of the S&Ls, it is a very cheap way of locking in your funds. Just a short time ago they were offering ½% bonus, which was still a very inexpensive method of assuring longevity of deposits, but the regulatory agencies forced them to cut the "bonus" in half! Certainly, as compared to what one may earn by taking advantage of grace days, daily interest and transfers, or by purchasing depositor savings certificates, the "5¼% bonus accounts" shouldn't be touched with an eleven-foot pole.

The second plan is available at many S&Ls across the U.S., and is offered by those paying only 4½% to 4¾% on their regular savings accounts. It is a six-month or one-year certificate, with a $1,000 or $5,000 minimum, that pays at a rate of 5¼% simple interest for the six months or year. If cashed in prior to the expiration date, only the 4½% or 4¾% is earned. As of Jan. 1970, S&Ls may offer 5¼% on 90 or more day certificates. 5¼% semi-annually yields 5.32% annually, compared to the yield of 5.13% from 5% compounded daily. Therefore, the actual increase in effective annual rate is only 0.19%, not 0.25%. These certificates are generally automatically renewable at whatever the then current interest rate is; the rate is not guaranteed, there are no bonus or grace days.

Compare this certificate with those offered by commercial banks: 5% interest compounded daily, yielding 5.13%; redeemable quarterly without penalty; interest rate guaranteed for five, ten, or fifteen years; no grace days.

Take your choice — 5.32% now with no guarantee of continuity, or 5.13% assured for some years and with slightly greater flexibility. After making the choice, compare with other opportunities now available. And *now,* for the new, dynamic, highly profitable opportunity. . . .

The United Security Account is so new that, as of this writing, it is only about eight years old! Yes, eight years. The currently used promotional literature was copyrighted in 1964, six years ago. At that early point in its history, it was able to boast of having more than 40,000 account-holders in all 50 of the United States and in 20 other principal nations of the world. The accounts are fully insured to $20,000 by the United States Government's Federal Deposit Insurance Corporation.

This new concept in banking is in the charge of men with the following credits to their past experience: President of a group of twelve insurance companies; Chairman of the Advisory Council of the National Association of Bank Commissioners; Federal Reserve and National Bank Examiner; Professor of Economics; Chief Examiner of Financial Institutions of the State of Illinois; President of American Bank & Trust Co. of South Bend, Indiana; Director of Mutual National Bank of Chicago; member of the Federal Reserve District Advisory Committee on Consumer Credit; Officer of the International Division of the Bank of America; and U.S. Vice-Consul in Germany and Finland.

This new type of account has been acclaimed in Fortune Magazine, The American Banker, the now defunct New York Herald Tribune, the Wall Street Journal, and the New York Post among others.

Of greater significance than the plaudits of the pundits is the space given to the concept by the Bankers' Forum column in the April 1968 issue of Matters of Interest, reprinted below in its entirety.

* * * * *

Innovation in our economy has been the life-blood of progress. The USA accounts described below are a unique innovation that could prove useful and profitable to our readers and subscribers, particularly for funds that have been kept in checking accounts and therefore not earning any interest. Although the bank is not an advertiser, the editors feel that the USA account is worthy of mention.

THE "MIRACLE" BANK ACCOUNT

It's the only one that works like a *checking account that pays interest* or a *savings account with checks.*

Most everyone has always wished he could get interest on his checking account, and most bankers would like to pay it, if it would expand their deposits. But every banker knows interest on demand (checking) deposits is absolutely impossible under the Federal Reserve Act as amended in 1933 and the Banking Act of 1935.

However, if you set up a line of check-credit against a savings account which naturally pays interest...and – *voila!* – you've done the impossible. That's just what happened seven years ago when an enterprising Chicago suburban bank, Citizens Bank & Trust Co. in Park Ridge, Ill., came up with its "USA" account (United Security Account). Not surprisingly, the bank has been gathering tens of thousands of new depositors all over the world with tens of millions of new deposit dollars.

The workings of the USA account are remarkably simple: deposits are held as ordinary savings paying 4% interest (since this is the current maximum the Federal Reserve permits banks to pay). But "USA Cheques" can be written any time on the entire balance as collateral. All new deposits first repay the "cheque-loans" created, and the rest simply adds to the interest-earning savings balance.

According to Citizens' Roderick MacArthur, who invented the plan: "Many USA accountholders also use a separate checking account for day-to-day money, but they say this is the ideal place for 'in-between money' – the money you *might* need in cash at a moment's notice but don't want to leave idle until you do. It's the *only* place where this kind of money can earn any interest."

Some USA depositors keep large balances simply for the peace of mind they get from knowing it's always instantly available by check. Others use it for day-to-day checking by making routine deposits of salaries, receipts, etc. Theoretically, there's a ¾%-per-month charge for the cheque-loans, but the routine deposits continuously "wash them out" during a free period up to 45 days before the charge is applied. Thus, they literally "do the impossible"; earn interest on an account that works exactly like a regular checking account.

Although in the hundred-million-dollar class, Citizens Bank wasn't geared to handle the flood of deposits that poured in by mail from all over the country after the plan was first introduced. Standard procedures were too slow, posting machines couldn't do the unusual bookkeeping, and conversion to new equipment slowed things even more.

"It was a rough time," says MacArthur, "but it was a long time ago, and we learned our lesson."

The bank closed the door on new accounts, put the whole thing on magnetic tape with a new 501 computer, and cautiously opened the door again. MacArthur says it runs like clockwork now, but they've been rationing new accounts ever since. He says a new block of accounts was recently released and is available at the moment.

USA accounts carry a unique guarantee in addition to all the standard ones: Whenever the Federal Reserve raises the interest ceiling, USA accounts are guaranteed in advance automatically to go to the new maximum no matter how high it is set. There is no minimum (or maximum) deposit limitation, checks are 15¢, and all other free account ser- vices are included.

(Editors note: As of Jan. 1970, Federal Reserve raised the inter- est ceiling to 4½%.)

* * * * *

At this point it should be noted that on the face of it, this type of account offers much the same as the bank credit card. Actually, it offers much *much much* more! Because this entire concept is unique and even unbelievable, and in order to be absolutely certain that no error would be made in describing it, permission was requested to reprint the USA Account material verbatim.

The request, dated March 26, 1968 read in part:

"I am in the process of preparing ... a full length book on popular banking. Offerings attractive to deposi- tors will be featured, and I expect to stress the apparent advantages of the USA account. Noting that much of your advertising material is copyrighted, and since it may be desirable to reprint all or part of both your space ads and fulfillment material, I shall appreciate it if you will send me permission from the bank to use any of their material. Full credit will, of course, be given to Citizens."

Prompt reply was received, dated April 2, 1968 as follows:

"Please be assured you have unlimited permission from this bank to reprint any part of current United Security Account advertising material. Credit need not be given.

> Very truly yours,
> Howard S. Hadley (signed)
> Director of Division"

First comes the advertisement placed by Citizens Bank and Trust Company, as it appears from time to time in such media as the New York Times.

Announce Expansion of Only Bank Plan that

Allows Checks and Top Interest at Same Time

New Block of "U.S.A." Bank Accounts To Be Opened to the Public

Citizens Bank has announced that a new block of its "United Security Accounts" is being released to the public. These are the only bank accounts in the United States that pay maximum savings interest on money that would ordinarily be kept earning nothing in a checking account for immediate access. The interest is paid on all money deposited, yet accountholders can write free checks on credit against the entire account. There is no minimum balance required, no service or check charges. It can, in effect, be used like a completely free checking account without affecting the interest earned.

The bank is in the $100,000,000 class with exceptional reserves and full F.D.I.C. insurance. All transactions are by postage-free mail.

Although "U.S.A." accounts are held by some 30,000 depositors throughout the U.S., new accounts have only been available at limited, fixed intervals, mainly to persons recommended by current accountholders. Now the bank says it will release a block of new accounts for applicants without recommendation.

During this limited period, anyone interested is invited to send, without obligation, for a free booklet describing the advantages of these accounts. The coupon below should be sent without delay.

-------------- **FREE BOOKLET COUPON** --------------

Howard B. Hadley, U.S.A. Director
Citizens Bank & Trust Co.
(Park Ridge) Chicago, Ill. 66645

    Please mail my Free Booklet with full information on how I can earn interest and write checks at the same time with your exclusive United Security Account plan.

Name _____

Address _____

City _____ State _____ Zip Code _____

CITIZENS BANK THE BIG BANK IN THE CHICAGO & HARE AREA

& TRUST COMPANY

assets over $100,000,000.00

(F.D.I.C.)

Once the coupon is sent in, the following letter, brochure (reprinted in part), account opening card, and sample check are received as fulfillment material together with prepaid airmail envelope. Read the letter and brochure carefully.

UNITED SECURITY ACCOUNT
DIVISION OF
CITIZENS BANK & TRUST COMPANY
CHICAGO, ILLINOIS 60648

Dear Friend:

Thank you for asking about a United Security Account.

I'm happy to tell you I can set aside an account for you. To take advantage of it, please return the validated application form with your deposit of $10.00 or more within 10 days. A second form is enclosed for your records.

If I do not hear from you in 10 days we will have to reassign your account. It is the only way we can be fair to the many applicants.

The United Security Account is the ONLY bank account in the entire United States that does both at once: Lets you earn the highest rate of interest on your savings, yet write checks whenever you want.

The mechanics are not complicated: The checks you write are simply loans. If you repay them with a new deposit by the middle of the following month, there is no charge. If you don't, there is a charge of ¾% per month until you do -- but remember, the money behind every check you write also continues to earn you full interest. In other words, all the money in your account earns full guaranteed interest, no matter how many checks you write. The checks are 15¢, and everything else is free.

The United Security Account plan has been carefully tested and proved over seven years under stringent governmental controls. Please read the enclosed folder now to see how thousands of other accountholders from coast to coast are truly "having their cake and eating it too" -- earning full interest on money which in effect remains in their pocket in the form of U.S.A. Cheques. Many of them also like the advantages of a convenient, confidential, out-of-town account.

Read how easy it is to combine the high interest earnings and checking privileges you get with no other account...anywhere. Then use the airmail envelope -- we pay postage both ways on all transactions. And please don't forget the 10-day time limit.

Meanwhile, if you have any questions, please write me. I look forward to serving you -- both personally and on behalf of Citizens Bank.

Sincerely yours,

Howard S. Hadley

HOWARD S. HADLEY
Director of Division

Only bank plan in America that pays you highest-rate interest and lets you write checks

Now, for the first time, you don't have to split your money between checking and savings. The United Security Account plan gives you the advantages of both. It's like adding check-writing to your savings account . . . or like getting maximum-rate interest on the balance in your checking account—money which never earned you one cent of interest before.

You literally "have your cake and eat it too" . . . you can now write checks up to the *full amount* of your savings *without losing a penny of your interest.*

Your United Security Account guarantees you *the very highest rate of savings interest paid by any bank in the United States,* (currently 4%, which is the maximum permitted by federal regulations). In addition, it is the only account that *also guarantees* you will *continue* to earn the highest rate no matter how high it may go. When it last increased, United Security Accounts were the only ones in the nation to go up automatically to the new maximum.

Deposits received through the 10th of any month earn for the entire month; your interest is compounded semi-annually.

But—unlike any other savings account—your United Security Account not only pays interest on your money but lets you continue to use it —all of it—as credit for writing checks any time you want . . . anywhere you may be. This means you earn top interest on money which, in effect, you keep right on carrying in your checkbook.

(Part of Brochure)

The Nation's Press:

"[of] all the savings institutions . . . the most imaginative plan . . ."
—*Fortune Magazine*

"Precedent-setting . . . . a depositor can, in effect, write checks against his savings . . ."
—*The American Banker*

"They [USA Cheques] are negotiable everywhere much like traveler's checks."
—*New York Herald Tribune*

". . . a service that seems to fill a real need for thousands of people . . ."
—*Wall Street Journal*

"By combining the advantages of both checking and saving, they have won wide favor with depositors in every state . . ."
—*New York Post*

U. S. Accountholders:

"Every time I get the statement showing my earnings on what would have been idle money, I thank [the friend] who told me about your U.S.A. plan."
—*A Washington, D.C., Analyst*

"We've never told you about the peace of mind we have from knowing we can write a check for thousands in an emergency . . . of the recent case where we paid a $400 hospital bill in Bangkok . . . with a U.S.A. check . . ."
—*An American Diplomat in Burma*

"My expenses jump each season and it helps to get this no-interest loan service without interrupting my savings earnings."
—*A Florida Citrus Grower*

"I always wanted an easily accessible, confidential . . . account that paid interest. My U.S.A. account is the best answer."
—*A Foreign Correspondent in Paris, France*

"Thanks [for the interest credit] . . . I never have trouble cashing U.S.A. Cheques and I travel all over the country."
—*An Alabama Wholesaler*

(Part of Brochure)

How Your Money Does Double Duty...

World's First to Give You Both:

Now, for the first time, you don't have to split your money between checking and savings. The United Security Account plan gives you the advantages of both. It's like adding check-writing to your savings account . . . or like getting maximum-rate interest on the balance in your checking account—money which never earned you one cent of interest before. You literally "have your cake and eat it too" . . . you can now write checks up to the *full amount* of your savings *without losing a penny of your interest*.

You're GUARANTEED Highest Interest...

Your United Security Account guarantees you *the very highest rate of savings interest paid by any bank in the United States*, (currently 4%, which is the maximum permitted by federal regulations). In addition, it is the only account that *also guarantees* you will *continue* to earn the highest rate no matter how high it may go. Every time it has increased, United Security Accounts have been the only ones in the nation to go up automatically to the new maximum. Deposits received through the 10th of any month earn for the entire month; your interest is compounded semi-annually.

...Even on the Money Behind Your Checks

Unlike any other savings account—your United Security Account not only pays interest on your money but lets you continue to use it—all of it—as a credit for writing checks any time you want . . . anywhere you may be. This means you earn top interest on money while, in effect, you continue to carry it all in your checkbook—even on the money behind checks you have already written.

(Part of Brochure)

Here's how you can earn interest and write checks at the same time

There's no magic; it's just a matter of making your money do double-duty: Every savings dollar you deposit automatically becomes credit against which you can write your special United Security Cheques. Your Cheques are then loans.

But they can be *free* loans . . . if you repay them with a new deposit by the 15th of the following month, there is no charge. If not, there is a charge of only ¾% per month or part of a month until you do. All new deposits first repay your cheque-loans (if any), and everything left over goes into your savings. Most important: *since your Cheques are never deducted from your savings, your account continues earning you full interest—even on the money behind every Cheque you write.*

Your savings interest is *guaranteed* to be the highest rate in the nation, not only now but in the future as well.

You bank the most convenient, confidential, fast way: by mail. Each Cheque paid costs you 15¢, and *everything else is free.*

(Part of Brochure)

Q *Are United Security Accounts insured?*

A *Absolutely.* United Security Accounts are fully insured to $15,000 by the United States Government's Federal Deposit Insurance Corporation. Citizens' own exceptional cash reserves and assets of more than $100,000,000.00 provide an extra measure of security. Depositing by mail is safe too; in more than 38 years no deposit mailed to Citizens has ever been lost.

Q *Are my United Security Cheques good everywhere?*

A *Yes.* Your Cheques are good anywhere in the United States and in all foreign countries. Each United Security Cheque clearly states that it is collectible at par through the Federal Reserve Bank of Chicago. They come in an exclusive U.S.A. Chequewallet with an official United Security Account Card which verifies your signature and Registered Account Number. This makes your Cheques self-identifying like Travelers Cheques.

Q *Are there any service charges?*

A *No.* Your registered U.S.A. Cheques, Chequewallet, Account Card, deposit forms, etc., are always free. So are your statements. The bank pays all postage. Since the ¾% Cheque-loan charge is not applied until the 15th of the *following* month, you always have from 15 to 45 days to replace the money with no cost whatsoever. Meanwhile, all your money continues earning maximum-rate interest, completely undisturbed.

Q *Are my Cheques ever deducted from my savings?*

A *Never* (unless your account closes completely). Your savings earnings are never disturbed by the Cheques you write. When it approved the other special privileges of these accounts, the Federal Reserve Board determined that United Security Cheques are not to be repaid by United Security savings. They are only repaid by another deposit; although of course you can still make *direct withdrawals* and use the money however you wish—just as with any other savings account.

Q *Do I have to keep a minimum balance?*

A *No.* There is no minimum or maximum (accounts range as high as $300,000) and no penalty for a small balance. Naturally, the larger your balance, the more interest you earn.

Q *How can Citizens offer United Security Accounts when other banks do not?*

A *Because Citizens Bank has always been a pioneer.* In 1929 it introduced complete banking-by-mail and has led in new bank services ever since.

Only Citizens Bank has perfected the many new forms and procedures required for a plan like United Security Accounts to meet strict Federal Reserve regulations and still keep operating costs within reason.

The most modern electronic techniques—magnetic checkreading and tape ledgering, closed-circuit TV signature verification, all transactions completely computerized—permit Citizens to process United Security Accounts at the high speeds needed to make the plan economically possible.

Only Citizens has spent seven years of research to develop United Security Accounts. So Citizens is the only bank that has the necessary experience and volume of business (with many thousands of U.S. Accountholders in all 50 states and 20 foreign countries); in short, Citizens is the only bank that can *afford* to offer such a plan.

(Part of Brochure)

Q *Do I get regular statements?*

A *Yes.* In addition to receipts by return mail for all deposits, Citizens sends you regular statements at the end of June and December showing the interest you have earned. You also receive monthly statements, if you have any activity other than deposits, showing all cheque-loans, charges, etc., in complete detail. Your cancelled U.S.A. Cheques, like those of a regular checking account, are returned to you monthly with these statements. And of course you get prompt, *personal* attention to any questions you may have at any time.

An example of how your United Security Account works to your advantage . . .

Suppose you have $5,000 in your account and you spend $100 with a U.S.A. Cheque. The bank pays it and charges you 15¢. You now owe $100.00 plus 15¢ for the Cheque. If you deposit this amount or more by the 15th of the next month, you incur no loan charge whatever. Your entire savings account (still $5,000) continues to earn 4% interest undisturbed. But suppose you decide not to redeposit until the third month. Then you pay ¾% per month (in this case, $2.25) for the loan plus 15¢ for the Cheque—a total of $2.40. Meanwhile, your savings have earned $50.00—*a net profit to you of $47.60.*

Q *Are new United Security Accounts always available to the public?*

A *No.* Much as the Bank would like to extend accounts to everyone requesting them, it is simply not always possible to meet the demand.

Citizens is the *only* United Security Account Accepting Bank for the entire United States. Programming time and computer availability alone make it necessary to release new blocks of accounts on a carefully planned schedule.

Except for rare vacancies, applications are accepted only after a new account block has been released. Whenever applications exceed the accounts available, they go on a waiting list which is given priority when the next block can be released.

Additional restrictions:
a. no deposit will be accepted in the name of a business firm operated for profit rather than the name of an individual.
b. No deposit will be accepted in the name of a minor.
c. No deposit will be accepted under a code or number only. If you use a professional name rather than your real name, please include your real name for the Bank's private files in case of death.

Q *How do I open my United Security Account?*

A *Simply fill out an application form* and mail it with your first deposit. If you don't have a form, Mr. Howard Hadley, the Director of the U.S.A. Division, will be glad to send you one. Please observe the time-limit in your invitation. Availability definitely cannot be guaranteed once this has expired.

On acceptance, your deposit will become an interest-earning savings account from the day of arrival, and an official Bank receipt will be sent you by return airmail. These savings will automatically create your line of Cheque-credit for the same amount, and you will receive your new U.S.A. Cheque-wallet with your Registered Account Card and first book of United Security Cheques.

But don't delay. Your United Security Account will *now* entitle you to checking privileges denied you by any other savings account; and on your regular checking account you are losing the interest you could *now* be earning—and losing more of it every day.

(Part of Brochure)

Exclusive Earning-Checking System ·U·S·A· Reg. U.S. Patent Off. 121,704

Offered only by

CITIZENS BANK & TRUST COMPANY

Park Ridge, Chicago, Illinois 60648, U.S.A.   Telephone: Area 312; NE 1-4270

Foreign Cables: CITIZENS-CHICAGO

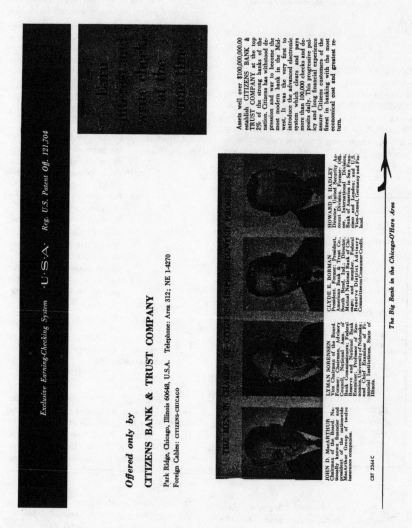

THE MEN IN CHARGE OF CITIZENS UNMATCHED MANAGEMENT

JOHN D. MacARTHUR, Chairman of the Board. Nationally known financier and president of the nationwide MacArthur Group of twelve insurance companies.

LYMAN SORENSEN, Vice Chairman of the Board. Former Chairman, Advisory Council, National Assn. of Federal Reserve and National Bank Examiner; Professor of Economics, University of Nebraska; and Chief Examiner of Financial Institutions, State of Illinois.

CLYDE E. BORMAN, President. Former President, American Bank & Trust Co., South Bend, Ind. Director, Mutual National Bank of Chicago; and member, Federal Reserve District Advisory Commission-Consumer Credit.

HOWARD S. HADLEY, Director, United Security Account Division, United Former Officer, International Division, Bank of America in San Francisco and London; and U.S. Vice-Consul, Germany and Finland.

Assets well over $100,000,000.00 establish CITIZENS BANK & TRUST COMPANY at the top 2% of the strong banks of the nation. Citizens has withstood depression and war to become the most modern bank in the Midwest. It was the very first to introduce the advanced electronic system which clears and pays more than 100,000 checks and deposits daily. This progressive policy and long financial experience assure Citizens customers of the finest in banking with the most economical cost and greatest return.

The Big Bank in the Chicago-O'Hare Area

CBT 2364C

(Part of Brochure)

APPLICATION FORM

CITIZENS BANK & TRUST COMPANY · Park Ridge, Chicago, Illinois 60648, U.S.A.
MEMBER FEDERAL DEPOSIT INSURANCE CORP. AND FEDERAL RESERVE SYSTEM ASSETS OVER $100,000,000.00

United Security Account DIVISION

ATTENTION: Mr. Howard S. Hadley, Director

NAME (Names): _____ OCCUPATION _____

Please Print

ADDRESS: _____ SOCIAL SECURITY No.: _____

COMMUNITY _____ STATE _____ ZIP CODE _____ TELEPHONE: Area. _____ No. _____

Label with validation number when applicable. Do not remove, but, whether label is correct or incorrect, please print your name and address on lines above.

If the validation label is not in my name (or if there is none), I was invited: ☐ by the Bank ☐ by the person named in the label ☐ by a current U.S.A. Accountholder whose name and address are:

_____

My application and first deposit are subject to my understanding on the back. *I am under no obligation to keep any minimum balance at any time and may withdraw my entire deposit free of charge by simple, signed request.*
My (our) signature(s) as it (they) will be used on United Security Cheques:

_____

_____

Once this material is received, many recipients follow through by opening an account.

Those who do not open an account receive a follow-up letter, again together with application form and prepaid airmail envelope. (See page 195.)

Those who opened accounts, received the letter reprinted in part on page 196. Note that the Matters of Interest article reprinted beginning on page 181 was distributed by the bank to a large mailing list.

It costs the bank a great deal for each new account, yet it is quite apparently well worth the cost, because the bank has continued to promote the account in national media.

As of five years ago, by the bank's own statement, there were over 40,000 USA account holders. Probably 200,000 people had read the above printed literature. As of today, possibly half a million people have been made aware of this unique and imaginative plan. Yet how many saw the truly golden opportunity that was being offered? For that matter, how many of the illustrious minds in the Federal Reserve, the Home Loan Banks, the advisory councils and the banking industry, *in toto,* recognized just how radical a change was being wrought? You, who have just been alerted to watch for and recognize opportunities in banking, how many of *you* recognize the jackpot?

Here's the crux of the matter:

While daily interest accounts pay interest to day of withdrawal, the USA account pays interest even after withdrawal — for 15 to 45 days. This doesn't sound like much at first glance, but that interest, plus daily interest accounts properly used, can yield upwards of 8% interest.

Even though by now you may be certain of the procedure followed, the theory will be outlined first, then the documented details of how depositors actually earned approximately 8% on their savings, even though the USA account then carried a nominal interest rate of 4%.

UNITED SECURITY ACCOUNT

DIVISION OF

CITIZENS BANK & TRUST COMPANY

CHICAGO, ILLINOIS 60648

AIRMAIL

Dear Friend:

Perhaps you have already mailed me your first deposit for the United Security Account I've been holding for you. But if you haven't, please let me remind you that your 10-day reservation period ends today.

Because I know how easy it is to put off things you seriously intend to do, I'll hold your account open for another 5 days. I'm sending this by airmail with another application and postage-free airmail return envelope to be sure I'll hear from you in time. Please send your initial deposit today (any amount over $10).

I'm sure you understand there can be no further extension; after the 5 days your account must be reassigned. Only a limited block of new accounts is available, and this is the only way we can be fair to all applicants.

Naturally we have a heavy demand because of the combined advantages you get with a U.S. Account that you get with no other bank account anywhere. It can be like getting maximum interest on a checking account or like writing checks on a savings account. Either way, you earn the guaranteed top rate of savings interest paid anywhere in the U.S. -- and you earn it on all your money, even on the money behind the checks you have written. Your account is fully insured up to $15,000 by the U.S. Government's Federal Deposit Insurance Corporation. You get confidential, fast, bank-by-mail convenience anywhere in the country postage-free. Your U.S.A. Cheques are self-identifying and negotiable anywhere.

UNITED SECURITY ACCOUNT

DIVISION OF
CITIZENS BANK & TRUST COMPANY
CHICAGO, ILLINOIS 60648

Dear Accountholder:

As promised in my last letter here is your Chequewallet and all you need to begin using your new United Security Account.

Your initial deposit became an interest-earning Savings Account the day it arrived. It was also used as collateral to establish your Cheque Credit for the same amount. You may now write U.S.A. Cheques against this credit. These cheques are paid with the bank's money. Your savings deposit is not touched and continues to earn highest-rate interest without interruption. If you repay your Cheque-loan by a new deposit on or before the 15th of the next month, there's no charge. If you don't choose to make a deposit by then, there's a charge of ¾% a month until you do.

You now have the combination of earning power and availability found in no other bank account today. Your personal account number, registered in your name, is printed on each Cheque, both in plain numbers for easy reading and in magnetic coding for reading by our computers.

Your Registered Account Card is enclosed in the window pocket of this envelope. Please sign the Card immediately and insert it behind the clear plastic window to the left of your Cheque pad. This serves to verify your signature and account number wherever you may be. If your Card or Cheques should ever be lost or stolen, notify the Bank at once; if it should occur abroad, use our cable address: "CITIZENS-CHICAGO."

I also enclose a pad of deposit forms with the same magnetic coding so that all your deposits can be electronically credited to your account -- plus two postage-free deposit envelopes. A new envelope will be sent with your official receipt for every deposit.

But first, the problem of uncollected funds must be reckoned with. Once a new USA account is opened with an initial deposit of $10, the new account holder receives a receipt for the deposit, a supply of deposit slips and checks, and a prepaid mailing envelope together with a letter and two printed flyers. They are reprinted on pages 198 and 199, with the single underlines those of the bank, while the double underlines have been added to alert the reader to restrictions that appear to knock the stuffings out of any plan to greatly increase earnings. The Sunday Punch is in the "Note on Uncollected Funds" which appears on page 199.

But you already know about uncollected funds, and that some uncollected instruments are accepted as cash. In the "Note" on page 200, the double underlines point up how liberal a policy the Citizens Bank has. The Sunday punch has turned out to be a creampuff — the perfect dessert to the meal of higher earnings . . .

In Example A it will be assumed that a USA account has been previously opened with a nominal deposit of $10, and is called Acct. No. 1 Acct. No. 2 likewise has been opened with $10 at a local savings and loan association paying 5% interest from day of deposit to date of withdrawal, compounded quarterly (DD-DW/QQ). In addition, deposits into Acct. No. 2 by the 10th of any month earn interest from the first of that month if held to the end of the quarter. (In this example, the bonus days at the end of each quarter are inconsequential.)

Example A

Step 1   Using a second party bank check, or other instrument acceptable as cash, deposit $10,000 into Acct. No. 1 on Oct. 2, by mailing early on Oct. 1.

Step 2   On Oct. 3, draw a $10,000 check on Acct. No. 1

HOW TO GET THE MOST FROM YOUR
UNITED SECURITY ACCOUNT

With ordinary savings accounts, depositors often fail to reach their savings goals because they hesitate to deposit when they can — a whole salary check, an entire dividend, etc. Instead, they put it in an ordinary checking account because they think they may run short and need the money in a hurry. But with a U.S. Account you never need hesitate to deposit any amount because you know that, if necessary, you can always use the money **immediately** simply by writing a U.S.A. Cheque.

If you have another savings account which does **not** let you write checks, you may now include it in your United Security Account. Just send the enclosed Free Transfer Form (with pass book or certificate if the other account uses one) in the postage-free deposit envelope. The Bank will handle your transfer free of charge and send you a new deposit receipt.

On the other hand, by making regular, routine deposits you can also use your U.S. Account like an ordinary checking account **but with the unique advantage of earning highest-rate interest on your residue money** — a new profit you can get with no other account. Regular deposits can continually wash out your Cheque-loans (and save loan charges) while the remainder automatically goes into your Savings to earn interest.

As with any checking account, U.S.A. Cheques must not be written for more than your Cheque-credit Available. A reasonable balance over Cheques written is always advisable to protect your interest profit plus your unique ability to write another Cheque if you need it.

The copyrighted design of U.S.A. Cheques and special inks protect you against counterfeiting or alteration. The paper contains a chemical which will change color if ink iradicator is used. If you should make a mistake in writing a Cheque, do not try to correct it. Destroy it and write a new one. There is no charge for destroyed Cheques.

Any deposit which arrives before the 11th of any month earns you interest for the entire month.

A NOTE ON "UNCOLLECTED FUNDS"

If your United Security Account Cheque Credit Available ever gets so
low that your next U.S.A. Cheque will be against the credit of your
last deposit, it's best to make sure this deposit is eight business-
days old (for deposit checks drawn on other banks in the United States)
or older. If your deposit is in checks on banks in a foreign country,
it is best to wait up to twenty business days, depending on the country,
before writing your U.S.A. Cheque. (You do not have to count time for
your deposits or cheques to get to this bank because the time each takes
will be about the same).

This does not mean your deposits are not credited immediately for earning
U.S.A. interest or repaying Cheque-loans. It simply means that for writing
checks, this bank, like every other bank in the United States, only accepts
deposits "subject to collection"; that is, subject to their actually being
paid by the other banks on which the checks are drawn. Until then they
are "uncollected funds".

We do, however, make exceptions for U.S. Accounts: If your deposit is in
"official" checks -- money order, payroll, cashier's, or government
checks, etc., -- you can safely write a U.S.A. Cheque against it right away.
But the safest thing is simply to keep enough balance in your account so
that your next cheque will not depend on your last deposit. In any ordinary
checking account, this balance might be "dead". But in your U.S. Account,
it not only lets you write cheques on "collected funds", it automatically
earns more interest money for you.

                              UNITED SECURITY ACCOUNT DIVISION

A NOTE ON "UNCOLLECTED FUNDS"

If your United Security Account Cheque Credit Available ever gets so
low that your next U.S.A. Cheque will be against the credit of your
last deposit, it's best to make sure this deposit is eight business-
days old (for deposit checks drawn on other banks in the United States)
or older. If your deposit is in checks on banks in a foreign country,
it is best to wait up to twenty business days, depending on the country,
before writing your U.S.A. Cheque. (You do not have to count time for
your deposits or cheques to get to this bank because the time each takes
will be about the same).

This does not mean your deposits are not credited immediately for earning
U.S.A. interest or repaying Cheque-loans. It simply means that for writing
checks, this bank, like every other bank in the United States, only accepts
deposits "subject to collection"; that is, subject to their actually being
paid by the other banks on which the checks are drawn. Until then they
are "uncollected funds".

We do, however, make exceptions for U.S. Accounts: If your deposit is in
"official" checks -- money order, payroll, cashier's, or government
checks, etc., -- you can safely write a U.S.A. Cheque against it right away.
But the safest thing is simply to keep enough balance in your account so
that your next cheque will not depend on your last deposit. In any ordinary
checking account, this balance might be "dead". But in your U.S. Account,
it not only lets you write cheques on "collected funds", it automatically
earns more interest money for you.

                              UNITED SECURITY ACCOUNT DIVISION

payable to yourself, and deposit this check into Acct. No. 2. Note that this USA account check is not an instrument that is acceptable as cash, and by the rules of the S&L into which it is deposited, as much as twenty days may be required for it to clear.

Step 3 On Nov. 3, withdraw from Acct. No. 2 the sum of $10,000.15 by tellers' check made out to you. Mail this check immediately as a deposit to Acct. No. 1.

On or about November 5th, the statement and cancelled check will be received for Acct. No. 1, showing a check-loan of $10,000 outstanding and the service charge of 15 cents. By having sent the deposit of $10,000.15 in Step 3, you have repaid the $10,000 check-loan and paid the 15 cents service charge for the check. This deposit, as repayment of loan, is recorded upon receipt into Acct. No. 1 on or about November 4th.

Step 4 On Nov. 5, draw a $10,000 check to yourself on Acct. No. 1, and deposit it that day into Acct. No. 2. (This is the same procedure as used in Step 2.)

Step 5 On Dec. 1, by tellers' check, withdraw $10,000.15 from Acct. No. 2 and mail immediately for deposit into Acct. No. 1. (This is the same procedure as used in Step 3.)

Step 6 On Dec. 10, repeat Step 4, by depositing a $10,000 check into Acct. No. 2.

Note that Steps 1, 3 and 5 have required a trip to the local S&L in which Acct. No. 2 is kept, while Steps 2, 4 and 6 were accomplished by writing and mailing the checks for deposit into Acct. No. 2, using prepaid mailers supplied by the bank.

If $10,000 had been deposited on October 1st into any account paying 4½% interest, total earnings on the $10,000 through the end of December would be $112.50. A 5% account would yield $125, while, if there were such animals, a 7% account would yield $175, an 8%, $200, and a 9%, $225.

Would you believe . . . that by executing Steps 1 through 6 more has been earned than a 7% account would have yielded? Would you believe . . . more than an 8% account? More than $200?

Here is the explanation of how a yield exceeding 8% has been accomplished.

1. Acct. No. 1 has earned a full $112.50 on the $10,000 deposited on October 2nd. Three separate times sums of $10,000 each were borrowed against the collateral of this account, but each time the loan was repaid prior to the 15th of the month following the loan — so the loan was free, with no interest charges whatsoever, with only a 15 cents charge for the use of each of the three checks. So, Acct. No. 1 has earned $112.50 (or, if the cost of the three checks is to be considered, $112.05 was earned).

2. Acct. No. 2 has earned interest, but this is somewhat more complex to figure. Interest has not been earned for the entire quarter, but only on the $10,000 for the following days:
Oct. 3 to Nov. 3 is 31 days
Nov. 5 to Dec. 1 is 26 days

Dec. 10 to Dec. 31 is figured as Dec. 1 to Dec. 31 because the grace days allowed in December permit interest from December 1st on the deposit made by the 10th and kept in through the end of the quarter. The interest collectable on Acct. No. 2 at 5% should be for 87 (or 88) of the 92 days in the quarter, for a total of approximately $118.00.

3. Therefore, the grand total of interest earned on the $10,000 available for deposit from October 1st through December 31st consists of $112.50 from Acct. No. 1 plus $118 from Acct. No. 2, or a total of $230.50 for the quarter, which is an annual rate of 9.22%. And if one wants to quibble about the 45 cents cost of the three checks drawn on Acct. No. 1, the interest rates still exceeds 9.2%

Before considering taking advantage of the opportunity to gain such an unbelievable return on insured deposits, follow the earnings history of the following actual accounts, with only the names changed.

(Editor's Note: In 1968, at the time of the following examples, the USA account paid only 4% interest. As of January 1970, this rate was increased to 4½%. Therefore, were these examples current, the net yield would be ½% higher than was earned in 1968.)

Each of the transactions described below can be followed on the transcripts of accounts as reproduced on pages 206 and 207.

1. On March 28 and 29, 1968, Edward Gray opened savings accounts with $20.00 at West Side Federal Savings & Loan Association in New York and with $25.00 at Citizens Bank and Trust Company in Chicago.

2. On April 3rd, Mr. Gray mailed a bank check made to his order for $3,000.00 (and endorsed by him for deposit only) to Citizens Bank for credit to his USA account. This deposit was credited to his account on April 4th, bringing his balance there to $3,025.00.

3. On April 5th, Ed Gray wrote out a United Security Check for $2,705.00 and deposited it into his account at West Side Federal. This deposit brought his account's balance at West Side to $2,725.00. It should be noted that this U.S. Check for $2,705 was drawn on the Citizens Bank as a cheque loan; the $2,705 was not deducted from his savings account balance at Citizens, but became a loan which, if repaid by May 15th, would incur no interest charges.

4. On April 13th, the check for $2,705.00 cleared the Citizens Bank. (Note that it took eight days after deposit for the check to clear in Chicago.) The account at Citizens now showed the $3,025.00 balance still earning interest, and, as of April 13th, a loan for $2,705.00 plus the check charge of 15 cents due to Citizens.

5. As of April 30th, the entire balance of $3,025.00 in the savings account in Citizens Bank had earned interest at the rate

of 4% for the entire month, since the deposit on April 4th fell within the ten grace days allowed for interest to be earned from the first of the month.

6. As of April 30th, at West Side Federal, $20.00 of the balance had earned interest at the rate of 5% for the entire month, with the balance of $2,705.00 having earned at that rate from April 5th to April 30th, or 25 days.

7. On May 7th, Mr. Gray withdrew $2,705.15 by *official check* from his account at West Side Federal and mailed the check to Citizens Bank to repay the cheque loan of $2,705.00 and the 15 cents check charge. This withdrawal left a balance of $19.85 in his account at West Side.

8. On May 8th, the $2,705.15 was credited to Ed Gray's cheque loan account at Citizens, wiping out the loan and check charge incurred in April. Note that there were no interest charges incurred, since the loan was repaid by the 15th of May.

9. On May 10th (following the procedure as shown in 3), Mr. Gray wrote a U.S. account check for $2,760.00 and deposited it into his account at West Side Federal. This deposit brought his account's balance at West Side to $2,779.85 ($19.85 previous balance as of May 7th plus deposit of $2,760.00). Again, note that this check for $2,760.00 was not deducted from Gray's savings account at Citizens, but carried as a loan which could be repaid without interest by June 15th. When the check for $2,760.00 cleared Citizens in Chicago, the account in Chicago showed the $3,025.00 balance still earning interest (at 4%), and a loan for $2,760.00 plus a 15 cents check charge.

10. As of May 31st, the entire balance of $3,025.00 at Citizens had earned interest at the rate of 4% for the entire month of May, as it had for the month of April.

11. During May, the account at West Side Federal earned interest as follows:
   a. From May 1st to May 7th interest at 5% on the balance of $2,725.00
   b. From May 7th to May 10th, interest at 5% on a

balance of $19.85

c. May 10th to May 31st interest at 5% on a balance of $2,779.85

12. On June 6th (as in 7.) Mr. Gray withdrew by official check from West Side the sum of $2,763.80 and mailed the check to Citizens in Chicago. Of this sum, $2,760.15 was used to repay the cheque loan of $2,760.00 and check charge of 15 cents. The balance of the check, or $3.65, was added to the savings account, bringing that balance to $3,028.65. This $2,763.80 withdrawal left a balance of $16.05 at West Side Federal ($2,779.85 − $2,763.80).

13. On June 8th, the deposit of $2,763.80 was credited to Ed Gray's account at Citizens, $2,760.15 of it being credited to the cheque loan account, and $3.65 being added to the savings account balance.

14. On June 10th (as in 3. and 9.), Gray wrote a U.S. account check for $2,340.95 and deposited it into the account at West Side in New York, bringing the balance to $2,357.00 ($16.05 previous balance plus $2,340.95). Note that this deposit was to earn interest from June 1st, since West Side Federal pays interest from the first of the month on deposits received by the tenth, if the funds remain in till the end of the quarter (June 30).

15. Late in June, Edward Gray decided that shortly he would need all of the cash from his savings accounts, so he informed Citizens Bank and Trust Company to credit his earned interest on June 30th, to withdraw $2,341.10 from his savings account to repay the cheque loan of $2,340.95 plus the check charge of 15 cents, and to remit the entire balance to him, closing the account.

16. He received a check in the sum of $717.81 from Citizens Bank and Trust Company, representing the remaining principal of $687.55 and $30.26 interest earned in the three month period.

17. On June 30th, Ed Gray's account at West Side Federal

showed a balance of $2,357.00 plus daily interest earned of $32.01, for a total of $2,389.01.

Edward Gray had deposited a total of $3,045.00 between March 28th and April 5th. For the three month period, he earned a total of $62.27 in interest from the two institutions, West Side Federal Savings & Loan Association in New York and Citizens Bank and Trust Company in Chicago. On $3,045 for three months (or one quarter).

at 4% the interest would be $30.45
at 5% the interest would be $38.06
at 6% the interest would be $45.67
at 7% the interest would be $53.28
at 8% the interest would be $60.90
at 9% the interest would be $68.91

Ed Gray earned interest of $62.27 or 8.2%. At the recently increased rates, interest earned would have been $66.27 or 8.7%. During the three months, he wrote three checks on the Chicago bank for deposit in the New York S&L, and made two check withdrawals from the S&L for deposit by mail in the Chicago Bank.

To help insure that all transactions from the previous case history are understood precisely, the actual record of the account at the New York S&L and statements from the Chicago Bank account are reprinted below, with each transaction keyed by number to the preceding explanation.

* * * * *

Passbook Record of Transactions of Ed Gray in Savings & Loan Association (paying 5% interest from day of deposit to day of withdrawal, with interest paid from the first of any month on deposits received by the tenth of the month, provided the funds remain till the end of the quarter DD-DW/QQ, 10 grace days each month if left to end of quarter.)

Date (1968)	Withdrawal	Savings (Deposits)	Dividend (Interest)	Balance	Keyed Reference
3/28		20.00		20.00	1.
4/5		2,705.00		2,725.00	3.,6.
5/7	2,705.15			19.85	7.
5/10		2,760.00		2,779.85	9.,11.
6/6	2,763.80			16.05	12.
6/10		2,340.95		2,357.00	14.
6/30			32.01	2,389.01	17.

Transactions of Ed Gray in the Chicago Bank (paying 4% interest semi-annually on savings accounts, and permitting interest-free loans against the collateral of the savings account, provided loans are repaid by the fifteenth of the following month).

Date (1968)	Deposits or Interest	Withdrawals or cheque-loans	Cheque Credit Available	Cheque Credit in Use	Working Savings Earning Interest	Keyed Reference
3/29	25.00		25.00	.00	25.00	1.
4/4	3,000.00		3,025.00	.00	3,025.00	2.
4/13		2,705.00 .15	319.85	2,705.15	3,025.00	3., 4., 5.
5/8	2,705.15		3,025.00	.00	3,025.00	7., 8.
5/16		2,760.00 .15	264.85	2,760.15	3,025.00	9.
5/31			264.85	2,760.15	3,025.00	10.
6/8	2,763.80		3,028.65	.00	3,028.65	12., 13.
6/14		2,340.95 .15	687.55	2,341.10	3,028.65	14.
6/30	30.26 (Interest)		717.81	2,341.10	3,058.91	15., 16.
		2,341.10 (Withdrawal)		.00	717.81	15.
		717.81 (Withdrawal)	.00	.00	.00	16.

Edward Gray's accounts were chosen as an example because they were easy to understand. No additional investment was made during the quarter, and Mr. Gray did not withdraw any funds for any purposes other than to transfer funds from one account to the other.

Other examples of use of the USA accounts in combination with daily interest-paying accounts were more confusing in that additional deposits were made during the period, and cheque loans were used to pay bills in addition to their use for deposits into the daily interest accounts.

Regretfully the people who had used these accounts preferred not having each transaction recorded herein. However, we had the opportunity to copy the entries from all passbooks, statements and checks, and computed the effective yield (or interest) for each of the three people. One had earned at the annual rate of 9.1%, the second at 8.9% and the third at over 10.4%!!! (At current interest rates, these figures would be ½% higher!)

A word of explanation is in order. The earnings of the latter three accounts exceeded 8½% because of one factor. Chequeloans were used to pay all major bills, as well as to make deposits in the savings and loan paying daily interest. As an example, when a check in payment of income taxes was sent out on April 12th, the sum of that check was no longer considered savings upon which interest could be earned. But interest continued to be earned in the working savings portion of the USA accounts on the entire amount of the cheque loan. By the fifteenth of the month after the cheque loan cleared, an additional deposit was made to the USA account rather than a withdrawal from the working savings, since such a withdrawal would have caused a loss of interest on that sum for the entire period from January 1st. (Referring back to the Citizens Bank and Trust Company literature, the reader will find that the working savings part of the USA account pays interest from date of deposit only if kept in the account to the end of the *semi-annual* period, the end of June or December.)

The theoretical explanation of the use of a check-loan savings account in combination with an account paying interest from date of deposit to date of withdrawal showed interest earnings at a rate of about 9.2%. The four actual accounts described above earned at annual rates between 8.2% and 10.4%, when the earnings from the bank and S&L were combined, or at the recently increased rates, earnings would have been between 8.7% and 10.9%.

The announcement by the New York Bank for Savings of "three new dividend extras" as of October 1, 1969 (as fully described in Chapter 12) makes possible a combined yield of over 9½% when this savings bank account is used in conjunction with the USA account. Deposits in the New York Bank can be made on the 8th, 9th or 10th of each month by Citizens Bank check-loan, while withdrawals by bank check from New York can be made the 1st, 2nd or 3rd of each month for deposit to Citizens Bank to repay check-loans. In this way, 4½% (compounded semi-annually) is earned from Chicago *plus* 5% (compounded daily) is earned from New York, to a theoretical net annual yield of 9.65%.

Naturally it is of something more than academic interest that depositors, ordinary people like the real person that our Ed Gray is, have been able to earn such high interest from their savings. However, we believe that what is of greater interest and importance is the precedent established by the issuance of the USA accounts by a commercial bank with the knowledge of and at least tacit approval of the state and federal regulatory agencies. This novel account seems to have firmly established the right of a commercial bank to issue interest-free loans to its savings depositors, using the savings accounts as collateral for the loans.

The acceptance by the regulatory agencies of the right of commercial banks to issue credit cards that offer interest-free credit also established an important precedent, but it should be noted that this form of credit is in no way tied to savings deposits. The holder of a bank credit card need not even be a depositor in the bank that issues the card.

The USA account pioneered by the Citizens Bank and Trust Company established the right of a bank to issue interest-free loans (as compared to credit for purchases) up to the full amount that an individual has on deposit in a savings account in their bank.

Although the specific name of the account may be registered as a trade mark and promotional literature may be copyrighted, an idea cannot be protected by patent. By virtue of the precedent set by the USA account and its operation over an eight-year period, it would appear the commercial banks are free to offer interest-free loans to potential or present savings account customers. If a bank offers loans up to 50% of one's savings account balance, the effective cost to the bank and yield to the depositor would be 9% as compared to the present cost and yield of 4½%. If the free loans were limited to one third of the savings balance, the cost and yield would be 6¾%.

It is manifestly unfair to expect the thrifty and retired to subsidize the savings bank and savings and loan industries. In the desire to keep mortgage interest rates low. If subsidy is necessary or desirable, let such subsidy come from the same sources as the other subsidies — from the entire country through the government, rather than from the owners of savings accounts.

The banking industry can well afford to give the thrifty a return on their investment high enough to offset inflation and to compensate them for the use of their money. If the plaint has been that banks are not permitted to increase interest rates due to government regulations, the USA account gives lie to their cry; they *do* have license to pay, as has been proven by Citizens Bank and Trust.

CHAPTER 18

Convenience, Flexibility, Safety And A Fair Return
Don't bank on it!!!!

Most of us bank our savings because of convenience, flexibility, the opportunity to gain a return and, above all, the safety offered by federal insurance.

Little, if any, fault can be found with the banking industry's offers of convenience and flexibility. But the return that can be earned from banked savings leaves much to be desired, while the safety of such savings is open to question.

Were banking permitted to operate in a free market, interest rates paid to depositors would rise quickly to the point where a realistic return on investment would be realized by the thrifty. But banking does not operate in a free market. It is comparatively free on its selling side — banks can and do charge whatever the laws of supply and demand allow on much of their loan business. But it is not free on its buying side — banks are subject to governmental-agency imposed interest *paying* ceilings.

In exchange for the obvious benefits of membership in the Federal Reserve System, the Federal Home Loan Bank System, the F.D.I.C. and the F.S.L.I.C., the savings industry has bartered away many of its prerogatives. Of utmost importance to the thrifty is the fact that the right to set interest rates to depositors is no longer vested in the banks, but rather in federal and state agencies.

In their righteous zeal to keep interest rates down, particularly mortgage loan interest rates, politicians and government have successfully legislated and ordained ceilings on interest rates permitted to be paid on the deposits of the people, the source of bank and S&L funds. However, they have not decreed that other commodities and services shall be likewise controlled, nor have ceilings been clamped on what rates banks can charge, so we wallow in a whopping inflation. The end result is that after interest is added to principal and income taxes paid, the buying power of the savings of the thrifty actually deteriorates – each month, each year and each decade.

The imposition of interest ceilings on the savings of the thrifty is manifestly unjust to the great mass of people who supply the hundreds of billions of dollars to the banking industry with which it may earn comparatively unrestricted high returns and profits.

Ceilings on interest rates paid by banks have forced the thrifty and retired to subsidize low mortgage interest, while all other subsidies are borne by the populace as a whole out of general government revenues. If subsidy is necessary to maintain low mortgage interest rates, why force the thrift-minded citizenry alone to foot the bill?

Even K. A. Randall, former Chairman of the Federal Deposit Insurance Corporation, in an address delivered at Ohio State University on October 17, 1967, stated that it is not the responsibility of supervisory authorities to set market rates paid on time money (savings). To do so would be to usurp the right of management to make policy decisions. *That right has been usurped,* and the thrifty are the poorer for it.

Just a month prior, Mr. Randall implied in a speech before the Savings Division General Meeting of the American Bankers Association in September, 1967, the time may soon be approaching when banks may lose their virtual monopoly as institutions in which the general public invests its funds in the expectation of a fair return thereon consonant with sound business practice. Once the mass of our citizenry awake to realize that their real return on savings is a negative quantity, banks may well lose their position of predominance as financial intermediaries.

Though the thrifty American has sacrificed much in return for some small modicum of safety for his funds, so too have the bankers. From its inception until the advent of FRB, FDIC, FHLBB and FSLIC, banking had been a ruggedly individualistic business. It was a good example of free private enterprise. (We take the term to be neither a dirty word nor a holy state of grace.) Today, American banking is an *oligopoly*.

> *Monopoly* is the exclusive control of supply and price of any commodity or service in a given market, *unhindered by free competition.*
>
> *Oligopoly* is control by a few competitors of supply and price of any commodity or service. Oligopoly is monopoly by an oligarchy.

And all of the federally insured savings industry is a mandated, legal oligopoly, controlled in fact by thirteen men — the seven members of the Board of Governors of the Federal Reserve System, the three members of the Federal Home Loan Bank Board and the three Directors of the FDIC.

Presidents of the United States have appointed them all. All are bankers, business men or both. Not one of them is representative of the hundred million who supply the three hundred thirty billion dollars of time deposits that make it all possible.

Banking consists almost wholly of the functions of borrowing and lending, and is substantially a middle-man function, providing (hopefully) a satisfactory service or reward at *both* ends. But neither service nor reward is satisfactory at *one* end.

Since 1935 the confidence of the American people in the banking industry as a safe repository for their savings and business funds has been re-established. This confidence is a direct result of the formation of the Federal Home Loan Bank System, and to an even greater extent, the inception of the Federal Deposit Insurance Corporation and the Federal Savings and Loan Insurance Corporation. Today, secure in the belief that our country guarantees the safety of savings, about a hundred million people have entrusted one third of a trillion dollars to American banks and savings and loan associations. The money represents their lifetimes' savings, their security, and their hope for the future. But their confidence may well be misplaced.

Is the depositors' confidence in the safety of their savings in banks and S&Ls really warranted? The strength of the federal insurance corporations is not what the public generally believes it to be. Neither the FDIC nor the FSLIC is backed by the full faith and credit of the U.S. Government. Both have only their own assets to rely on, plus the availability from the U.S. Treasury of $750 million to the FSLIC and $3 billion to the FDIC.

The Comptroller General in his report to Congress in 1964 seriously questioned the liquidity of the Federal Savings & Loan Insurance Corporation.

The available reserves of both the FDIC and the FSLIC are grossly insufficient to protect our savings in the event, albeit unlikely, of a major national recession or depression. Remember that the word "Federal" in their titles does not mean that our deposits are protected by the full faith and credit of the United States Government.

Should there be a major economic crisis, a recession or depression despite all of the safeguards against such occurrences, we may well fear for the liquidity of both the FDIC and the FSLIC.

Fire insurance operates on the basis that fires will be widely scattered, and that even should an entire area burn, nationwide conflagration need neither be anticipated nor protected against.

With deposit insurance, we can enjoy no such assurance. The safety of savings *is* assured as long as banks and S&Ls have only occasional failures. However, should there be a national economic crisis, should prices and values tumble from their over-inflated perches, even if bank failures never reach the magnitude of those of the early thirties, it is not only possible, but it is probable that both of the federal insurance corporations would be unable to pay out completely on insurance should panic ensue. Without attempting to unravel the complex picture of the insuring agencies' real liquid assets, we would estimate that each hundred dollars of deposits is protected by less than a dollar and a half of insurance funds. This ratio is more than adequate to protect depositors in normal times, but even ten times that amount of insuring funds could prove to be grossly insufficient in times of economic disaster on a national scale.

Should not the Congress consider backing the FDIC and the FSLIC with the full faith and credit of the U.S. Government?

Without organization and leadership, the thrifty (half the nation) are powerless to right the wrongs. In the absence of strong union, individual depositors can ameliorate their plight by exploiting the loopholes and devices which permit higher returns. And if the loopholes are closed, they still have a further alternative.

We can buy U.S. Treasury Bills that offer yields up to 7% or 8% and U.S. Treasury Bills *are* backed by the full faith and credit of the United States. And 7% is 40% more than 5%. 8% is 60% more than 5%.

We can also buy government agency and commercial paper at yields of up to 8¼% and 10% respectively. Although this type of investment is not insured, the reserves of many corporations offering such returns compare favorably with the reserves of many banks and insuring agencies combined. Any good stock-brokerage house can supply the necessary information.

The purchase of both Treasury Bills, government agency and commercial paper in the open market bypasses the banking industry. If the banking industry cannot or will not offer their source of money-supply an equitable return on investment, banks deserve to lose their position of preeminence as financial intermediaries.

In these times of Buy Now, Pay Later, the cause of the apathetic thrifty has been unchampioned, unheralded and unsung. For the safety of federal agency insurance on their savings, the populace has sacrificed a major portion of the real value of their savings. And the safety for which they have made this sacrifice is not that assured.

It is not our purpose to undermine the depositor's confidence in the safety of his savings. Under all but the most extraordinary circumstances, he may sleep easy with the assurance that his funds are in no danger whatever from loss due to theft, recession, or even isolated bank failures.

But there's another kind of loss, far more insidious — the loss of dollar *value* because of inflation; the loss of earnings because of an unconscionably low interest rate virtually imposed on the depositor with government approval; the loss of representation among legislators largely unconcerned about the plight of the apathetic depositor.

For these losses, the depositor has alternatives. As the preceding pages have demonstrated, there are ways of doubling, and perhaps tripling and quadrupling his yield on savings, with minimal or no risk. And there is a way — the *only* way — for the depositor to make his impact felt on the legislative and regulatory bodies so that he is no longer subject to wilful discriminatory practices, no matter under what rationale they are committed. That way, of course, is by uniting with other depositors throughout the nation.

Postscript

HOW TO TURN A BANK RESTRICTION INTO YIELDS OF OVER 18%!

Some depositors who had taken advantage of Citizens Bank advertised benefits as described in previous editions of this book (see Chapter 17) received this letter from the Bank's director:

"We have reviewed the activity on account number _____
and, as a result, have decided to close this account effective
_____. At that time, interest due will be credited,
any cheque-credit in use retired, and our cashier's check for the balance will be sent to you."

A later version of that letter is more informative:

"In analyzing the activity on your account number _____,
we note it is being used to rotate substantial sums on a systematic basis. This serves to deny the bank investment funds to meet the interest liability. Such general usage can constitute an unsound banking practice which, of course, is prohibited by Federal and State bank regulations. Accordingly, this is notice under the Standard Savings Rules that the net balance standing to your credit will be returned to you by cashier's check on _____.
"Interest due will be credited pro rata to that date and any cheque-credit in use retired.
"Please let me stress that this action is taken as a uniform measure and is not a reflection on you in any manner whatsoever."

Recently, this restriction was added to Citizens Bank's brochure:

"No account will be maintained consisting of large sums (like $5,000, $10,000, etc.) which are rotated on a systematic schedule between this and other financial institutions."

This need not be a drawback. The canny depositor can take advantage of the new restriction to obtain a yield of *over 18%* on some of his savings. Here's how it can be done:

Let's assume that your family's monthly bills—rent, mortgage, utilities, food, clothing, credit card charges, and so on—total about $800. You pay your bills at the end of the month. You receive your paycheck weekly on Fridays. You have a day of deposit to day of withdrawal (DD-DW)) savings account at a local bank or S & L, and you maintain the minimum balance required, if any, to earn daily interest.

You can pay your bills at the end of the month if you deposit $200 in your DD-DW account each Friday. You make your first $200 deposit, say on Friday, January 7th, and the next two on Fridays, January 14th and 21st. On the 28th, you withdraw the $600 from your savings account and deposit it, together with $200 from that day's paycheck, into your checking account, so that you can pay your bills at the end of the month. This is what you would earn from day of deposit to date of withdrawal at the rate of 4½%–5%:

$$
\begin{aligned}
\text{Jan. 7th} - \text{28th} &= 21 \text{ days} \times \$200 \\
\text{Jan. 14th} - \text{28th} &= 14 \quad " \quad \times \$200 \\
\text{Jan. 21st} - \text{28th} &= \underline{7} \quad " \quad \times \$200 \\
\text{Total} &= 42 \text{ days} \times \$200 = 8400 \text{ dollar days} \\
&\quad \text{at } 4\frac{1}{2}\% - 5\%
\end{aligned}
$$

This is equivalent to interest on $8,400 for 1 day, or on $840 for 10 days, or on $280 for 30 days (1 month).

Take the following steps and you can *quadruple* that yield:

Step 1—If you don't already have a United Security Account (USA account) obtain one. Keep a small balance.

Step 2—On the first Friday of the month (January, the 7th) deposit $200 into your USA account.

Step 3—On the next Friday (the 14th) deposit another $200.

Step 4—On the next Friday (the 21st) deposit another $200.

Step 5—On the final Friday of the month (the 28th) deposit another $200. You now have added a total of $800 to your USA account, enough to pay your bills.

Step 6—On Monday (January the 31st) write and mail USA checks totaling $800 to pay your bills. When these checks clear—in *February*—your account will show that you had used $800 in cheque-credit *during February*. Repay the $800 by the 15th of March and it's interest-free.

Step 7—On the following Friday (February 4th), deposit $200 into your local DD-DW savings account.

Step 8—Deposit $200 into your DD-DW account on the 11th, 18th and 25th. During the month of February you will have deposited $800.

Step 9—On February 29th withdraw that $800 from your DD-DW account and deposit it (plus any check charges) to your USA account to repay the $800 carried as cheque-loans. Your USA account then shows $800 in working savings (plus your original balance), and $0 in cheque-loans.

With the USA account this is what you earned at 4½%:

Jan. 7th – 28th = 21 days × $200
Jan. 14th – 28th = 14   "   × $200
Jan. 21st – 28th = 7   "   × $200
Jan. 28th – 28th = 0   "   × $200

Sub-total = 42 days × $200 =   8,400 dollar days
at 4½%

PLUS

Jan. 28th – Feb. 29th
= 32 days × $800 = 25,600 dollar days
at 4½%

Total =   34,000 dollar days
at 4½%

This is equivalent to interest on $34,000 for 1 day, or on $3,400 for 10 days, or on $1,133 for 30 days (1 month). Had you used *only* your DD-DW account, you would have ended up, remember, with 8,400 dollar days at 4½–5%, which is equivalent to interest on $8,400 for 1 day, or on $840 for 10 days, or on $280 for 30 days (1 month). It's obvious that, *with the combined use of your USA and DD-DW accounts, your earnings are more than four times as much as obtained through the use of just your DD-DW savings account.* Compared to DD-DW yield of 4½% to 5%, your USA yield is equivalent to *over 18%*.

You can continue these exceptional earnings month after month. Here's how:

Step 10—On February 29th, send out USA checks for a total of $800 to pay your February bills. These payments are carried as cheque-loans in March, and are interest-free if repaid by April 15th.

Step 11—Each Friday during March, deposit $200 to your local DD-DW savings account.

Step 12—At the end of March, send $800 (plus check charges) from your

DD-DW account to your USA account to repay the $800 of cheque-loans. And so on—following the same procedures monthly.

Suggestion: To help avoid the possibility of your USA account being closed out on you, deposit some *regular* savings in it in addition to the amount used to pay bills.

Caution: Many readers have suggested that the loan privileges of a USA account are better than those offered by bank credit cards (at 12%–18%), because the USA account charge is only 9%. The loan privileges of a USA account are *not* better.

When you borrow on your bank credit card, you borrow the bank's money. When you borrow from a USA account, *you're really borrowing your own money*. The USA account pays you 4½% (and then only if the money remains in the account until the end of the semi-annual period). When you borrow, you pay the bank double the rate they pay you. Your cost is 9%, less the 4½% paid to you, or a net cost of 4½%—*for using your own money*. You're better off withdrawing funds from your DD-DW savings account. You'll get the money—and save that 4½%.

Something new for the thrifty was developed a few years ago which bears mention because of its success. In this new way of saving, your account is not insured by the F.D.I.C. or F.S.L.I.C., but the safety of your funds is reasonably well assured since the portfolio consists solely of obligations of the U.S. Government and its agencies. Investments yield earnings that have run in the area of 7% or more, and the operation is quite similar to day of deposit to day of withdrawal accounts. Complete information about this novel form of saving may be obtained by requesting a prospectus and descriptive literature from the Fund for U.S. Government Securities, Inc., 423 Seventh Avenue, Pittsburgh, Pa. 15219.

* * * * * *

A final word. No bank rules last forever. Some bank advertisements can be misleading. The guiding principle in estimating your earnings on most savings accounts is DON'T BANK ON IT! That's why this book was written: to give you the facts so you can see through the advertising copy, adjust to rule changes, and get the most from your savings—despite the uncertainties and ambiguities of some bank practices. We hope that you will be able to make savings deposits you *can* bank on.

—Martin J. Meyer, Dr. Joseph M. McDaniel, Jr.
January 4, 1972